rhododendrons
camellias and
magnolias
2012

Royal
Horticultural
Society

Published in 2012 by
the Royal Horticultural Society,
80 Vincent Square, London SW1P 2PE

ISBN 978 1 907057 30 4

Designed for the RHS by Sharon Cluett

Edited for the RHS by Simon Maughan

Honorary Editor for the Rhododendron,
Camellia and Magnolia Group
Pam Hayward

Opinions expressed by the authors are not
necessarily those of the Royal Horticultural
Society

Printed by Page Bros, Norfolk

COVER ILLLUSTRATIONS
FRONT COVER: *Camellia* x *vernalis*
(Sally Hayward)
BACK COVER (*TOP*): *Magnolia acuminata*
(Sally Hayward)
BACK COVER (*BOTTOM*): *Rhododendron
stenopetalum* 'Linearifolium' (Sally Hayward)

Royal
Horticultural
Society

Contents

Chairman's Foreword

ANDY SIMONS

MAINTAINING THE RATE and the quality of Rhododendron, Camellia and Magnolia group activities is something that has troubled me greatly over the year. Following my comments in the introduction to the last journal, whilst we are superficially strong with our regional activities, tours and particularly the publications, it is clear to me that this success is actually very fragile. As I have said before, in many ways the Group is functioning at a professional level, indeed at the sort of performance not seen since the RHS itself stepped back from the production of the journal some 40 years ago. I am concerned that this level of output is unsustainable due to the burden it places on the Group committee and a handful of ordinary members. It has proven very difficult, and on occasion impossible, to start new activities for the Group since we have simply been unable to find someone to lead the activity.

These problems are compounded by the logistic difficulties and cost of holding committee meetings. With a nationwide group it is essential that the committee is drawn from as far afield as possible, in order that the views of the membership can be adequately captured and acted upon. However, the cost of travelling to a London flower show to attend a meeting is now becoming problematic even when advance purchase arrangements are made. The committee has acted very prudently in managing these travel expenses and it has been possible to limit the cost against the Group's capital to a degree that leaves me pleasantly surprised. It has been suggested for our committee and a range of other direct RHS committees that electronic meeting tools such as teleconferencing should be adopted. We in the Group committee will be experimenting with such a capability in the coming year, however this throws into relief an insurmountable problem concerning 'virtual gardening' that I shall return to later. In short, we, as the entire Group, will need to consider very carefully how we take forward our activities in future years. Whilst I am not suggesting any immediate or precipitate changes, I strongly believe we need a plan by which we transition from the present situation of saturating a handful of willing people to something more sustainable for a group such as ours in the 21st century. I genuinely welcome any comments on the performance of the Group and suggestions in this area would be of particular benefit. The topics you may wish to consider include the use of external professional assistance, with the associated costs that would involve or the introduction of a range of less formal activities, methods of communication or publishing? I, like many of you, am uncomfortable with the vogue of change for change's sake; however we must be prepared for a changing future.

The problem with the internet and the 'cyber world' is that it can only provide an impression of plants or gardening. Gardening and horticulture are hands-on activities: the 'feel' necessary to achieve a successfully grafted magnolia, for example, cannot be relayed through a web page or even a video clip. Collecting gardening books is a consuming obsession of mine, one I suspect many of you share to a less intense level (*or at least I hope so*) but nobody, either now or in the past, seriously believes that a gardening book, no matter how well produced, can be a substitute for the real thing such as a garden visit or a trip into the wild. Yet it is often portrayed that all the information necessary for a plant, a gardening technique or the other things we need to communicate can be achieved through the internet. Perhaps other areas of interest can be seamlessly transferred to the computer world but gardening cannot; the internet can be a tool to help gardeners but in reality only a poor one. The real problem that this underlying truth exposes is that as the world becomes more computer based, reality becomes more

RHODODENDRON 'HYPERION' one of the Group's Hardy Hybrid Collection plants at Ramster
                                    SALLY HAYWARD

expensive. You may ask what I am talking about but consider the difference in the cost of viewing a video diary of a garden visit on the internet compared with that of actually travelling to that garden, paying the entrance fee, buying lunch and then travelling home! Perhaps we should surrender and establish a 'virtual' magnolia garden complete with virtually grafted magnolias? What does a 'virtual' rose smell like?

On the plant front itself, the Late Rhododendron Competition I promised last year seems almost certain to proceed at the RHS Garden of Harlow Carr – the RHS Shows Department have been very forward leaning on this issue as have the garden, although we do not expect it to commence until 2013. Let us hope it becomes a success similar to the Main Rhododendron Competition at Rosemoor. The RHS shows department do not get the praise they deserve and are often unfairly criticised for not pleasing all of the people all of the time.

I have cause to mention one class at the Main Rhododendron Competition as it was so impressive; it was as though the entries had been imported via time machine from one of the great gardens of the 1930s. This class was so full of the different forms of *Rhododendron* Loderi Group it took the judges as long to look at them as it would normally have done to judge 10 or 20 classes.

I think we did see a break in the performance of the main magnolia varieties, however. Although not a bad year, the spring weather did not permit the great flowering season to which we have become so accustomed. The season was early enough to cause some show entries to be mistimed, although the Cornwall Garden Society spring show at Boconnoc, benefited by being just a few weeks earlier.

To conclude on plants, many of you will not have noticed the explosion of new camellia species coming into cultivation across the world. In the UK we are pretty stuck with a limited range of camellia varieties, let alone species, but I recently saw seed from half a dozen species that are not mentioned even in the latest literature. It is unclear to me what is fuelling this expansion. Is it genuine discovery, a different botanical approach to the nomenclature or something else? Many of these newer varieties are tropical or at least not considered fully hardy; perhaps the older plant hunters did not cover the tropics as closely as the temperate regions? Even if not hardy, the genetic opportunities seem to have grown out of all recognition. Consider, only a few years ago a camellia enthusiast would have been aware of just one or two yellow flowered species, now we see entire chapters describing many forms and species. I predict that the next generation of camellia growers will have a vast increase in the forms they are able to grow – a slightly scary situation actually – it's complicated enough already!

Finally, and as always, I am keen to hear from you all on any issue that you think I should be addressing or doing better, or anything you feel the Group needs to escalate into the central RHS itself. You may not always get an instant answer but I will read it.

THE LODERI GROUP CLASS at the 2011 Main Rhododendron Competition at Rosemoor

SALLY HAYWARD

Editorial

PAM HAYWARD

RUNNING MY EYES down the list of articles which together make up the 2012 edition of the yearbook, I was suddenly, and quite unexpectedly, really moved. The combination of authors and their subjects came into sharp focus and reminded me how very fortunate we students of our three genera are to have the actions and experiences of such a long continuity of remarkable people to draw upon to increase our understanding and enrich our gardens.

Not surprisingly, my first thoughts went to the plant hunters who made and make it possible for us to grow the wealth of species currently available. The impact of Joseph Hooker's rhododendron collections is legendary but ponder for a moment just how influential they have also been in terms of hybrids, even now. Perhaps his introductions of *Rhododendron arboreum* are the most important example and Tony Schilling's fine concluding article on the species celebrates the legacy of Hooker and his successors – Tony is right there among them of course. Consider also the case of the striking red form of *R. multicolor* (*R. curtisii*): collected once by Charles Curtis between 1880 and 1882, treasured, then lost, and over a century later rediscovered by a dedicated collector keen to prove it was more than just an exotic entry in Curtis's Botanical Magazine. This edition serves as a tribute to the continuous rich thread of exploration and endeavour from which we all benefit.

The Magor family of Lamellen have long been associated with rhododendrons and our specialist society. Probably not fully appreciated, though, is just how important EJP Magor was in terms of personally facilitat-ing the distribution of newly-collected rhododendron species to enthusiastic growers. His particular initiatives in sharing both seed and his wealth of experience in raising rhododendrons with the pioneering American nurserymen of the time are of great historic significance. John Hammond's marvellous account of the Magor legacy gives a fascinating insight into the golden age of rhododendrons and gentleman gardeners, the ups and downs of the twentieth century for Lamellen and its revival at the hands of the present generation in the twenty-first.

What of the hybridisers, past and present? The continued pursuit of perfection or novelty is another sparkling thread running through our history. Gustave Croux represents the classic nurseryman entrepreneur – keen to develop new cultivars, produce plants for the gardens of the day and demonstrate his prowess at exhibition: a marvellous representative of that group of individuals generating hardy rhododendron hybrids in number at the turn of the twentieth century.

Felix and Mark Jury, working considerably later than this, with vireya rhododendrons, nevertheless share that same spirit, striving to create the superior but with the pragmatic approach that commerce dictates – and which surely is to be praised since only the really worthy plants survive rather than the mediocre which sentimentality can all too often cause gardeners to tolerate and retain in their gardens.

Dennis Ledvina is a hybridiser of equal dedication but altogether different goals. His aims are non-commercial and tailored to the development of hardiness and stature suited to modern gardens across a wide variety of climates, but in working so adventurously with the whole range of genus *Magnolia* and its hybrids he is introducing colours and forms never seen before on the lists of magnolias available to us.

It's not only the hybridiser's art which brings a better plant into our gardens: the ruthless selection and assessment of different cultivars of a particular species by specialist horticulturists and nurserymen also serves the ordinary gardener seeking the best. Kevin Parris has proved himself ably qualified in this respect, having raised one of the most successful recent introductions of *Magnolia grandiflora* – *M. grandiflora* 'Kay Parris'. His detailed comparative study of the various cultivars of this species is long overdue and very welcome in this edition. Having been overlooked as a plant for the modern garden, this account will surely open eyes to its creative versatility in a variety of settings.

And what of those who help us to understand the science behind our chosen genera? Constantly changing techniques and methodology have broadened our scientific knowledge beyond all measure since our Group started out, but so elevated has some of the written material become that even attempting comprehension is often unwise and best avoided! However, when this information is directly confirmed by our own experiences and observations, it is well worth persevering with terminology and concepts. Rhododendron competition attendees of recent years are sure to have noticed that a handful of hybrids are frequently among the awarded entries; keen observers will have looked more closely and recognised that these varieties have a certain 'something' about them – larger, fuller trusses, intensity of colour and lustrous foliage which grabs attention. Consider *R.* 'Grace Seabrook', *R.* 'Horizon Monarch' and *R.* 'Phyllis Korn' – get the picture? Now read the impressive article put together jointly by John and Sally Perkins and scientists at the University of Coimbra, Portugal to find out exactly what accounts for this special quality in certain rhododendrons: a science lesson undoubtedly but a real aid to understanding how superiority in hybrids is not all down to chance.

Then there are those who are busy developing particular skills, delving into the past in order to help us recognise what we have in our old gardens in the present so that it can be saved and treasured for the future. Bee Robson has been honing her camellia curatorial skills since working with the heritage collection at the Lost Gardens of Heligan. An acknowledged expert and passionate researcher, the account of her 2010 trip to Brittany is a practical demonstration of her talents and dedication.

Of course without the enduring practical skills and experience required to maintain this bounty of plants over time we would have no legacy to protect. How blessed we are then to be able to benefit from individuals such as Jennifer Trehane who has dedicated her life to genus *Camellia* and who gives of her knowledge so freely. Her crisp and succinct article on keeping camellias under control is uncompromising and delivered in her refreshing, inimitable style and much to be enjoyed!

Head Gardeners, too, figure greatly in our history and the name of Philip Tregunna is on the list of the very finest to have achieved that role. Charged with the care and development of Caerhays Castle Gardens for 40 years, he rose from the ranks, excelled and surpassed the position of Head Gardener, earning recognition as a skilful hybridiser of all three of our genera, with notable success. Charles Williams demonstrates his obvious respect and affection for this very able man in a particularly fond tribute which clearly reveals the bond which existed between them.

Having looked back and cherished the richness of our past, and highlighted its value to the present, what are we passing on to the future? Well, it is an especial pleasure to include in this edition two examples of how this fine institution of ours is investing in people who might become the plant hunters and scientists of tomorrow. A few years ago the Group and individual members undertook the sponsorship of PhD student, Tobias Marczewski, studying at the University of Edinburgh. Tobias completed his doctoral thesis in 2011 and an article based upon it is published in this yearbook.

Tom Clarke is the first professional gardener the Group has supported to travel into the wild to study rhododendrons in their native habitat. Many have already benefited from the lectures Tom has given about his trip to Arunachal Pradesh but now we can all enjoy his account in print.

The ability to provide young people, such as Tobias and Tom, with an opportunity to further their knowledge and develop skills is something of which we should all be immensely proud.

Once again, it has been a privilege to work with so many eminent authors and contributors and I thank them all for their time and effort in bringing this edition to publication. I hope there is something of interest for everyone.

The Jury vireya legacy

ABBIE JURY

THE ORIGINAL PLANT OF FELIX JURY'S FORM OF *RHODODENDRON MACGREGORIAE*
collected in New Guinea in 1957

ABBIE JURY

BACK IN THE 1950s, when Felix Jury first became interested in vireyas, they were pretty much unknown in New Zealand, with few enthusiasts internationally.

Felix started raising from seed and trying controlled crosses but at that time he was just after anything that was new and therefore interesting; there was so little raw material to choose from in those early stages. He named maybe a dozen and, with the passage of decades, about four of that dozen have stood the test of time very well and may still be around in another 30 years' time. Unfortunately, the finer details of his crosses were never recorded so it's not possible to state with certainty which were Felix's own crosses and which came from seed sent to him from overseas and were therefore just raised and selected by him. We do know that the Australian, Tom Lelliot was particularly generous with seed and there were others from that country.

In 1957, Felix went collecting in the highlands of New Guinea and brought back several plants of enduring interest. *Ficus antiarus* remains the most asked about tree in our garden and *Schefflera septulosa* is one of the most beautiful members of that plant family you will ever see.

RHODODENDRON 'GOLDEN CHARM'   ABBIE JURY

His form of *Rhododendron macgregoriae* is still rated as one of the best in circulation and, astonishingly, the original plant is still surviving. This is an achievement because vireyas are not noted for being long-lived in our climate. It was that plant of *R. macgregoriae* which gave rise to one of Felix's best cultivars – *R.* 'Golden Charm' (*macgregoriae* x Princess Alexandra). We still rate it highly after several decades. The foliage is dark and glossy, the new stems are red, the habit is compact and healthy and the many flowers, while relatively small, are in good sized heads and attractive apricot to orange tones. It is also relatively hardy.

With the benefit of hindsight, we now wonder whether Felix's other two notable *R. macgregoriae* hybrids, *R.* 'Buttermaid' (*aurigeranum* x *macgregoriae*) and *R.* 'Orangemaid' (*laetum* x *macgregoriae*) might not in fact be from Lelliot seed, raised and selected by Felix. There is also the possibility that he may have been sent pollen. Mark is unsure whether Felix had *R. aurigeranum* at that stage but is certain that he did have *R. laetum*.) The *R. macgregoriae* parentage shows dominance in both the flower form and colouring of these selections but hybrid vigour makes them more reliable and tidier garden plants.

R. 'Queen of Diamonds' (*viriosum* x *macgregoriae*) was indubitably Felix's own cross, a pink version

this time but rather too tall and leggy to be of great merit. [Apparently *R. viriosum* was misidentified for 70 years as *R. lochiae*. Most records use the *R. lochiae* name when it appears that they are all, in fact, *R. viriosum*. I will defer to those with a great deal more expertise in this matter and have accordingly changed to using *R. viriosum*.]

R. 'Satan's Gift' (*konori* x *zoelleri*) and *R.* 'Silken Shimmer' (*konori* x *Dr Herman Sleumer*) were selections from Australian seed, raised by Felix. These were spectacular for their day, being big and lush, colourful and fragrant. *R.* 'Satan's Gift' is the stand-out plant which has passed the test of time and is still a wonderful performer. The name amuses us – Felix was a completely non-religious man and to him, Satan merely evoked hot colours. Over the years, more devout nurseries have clearly had a problem with the name and this cultivar has been marketed variously as 'Jury's Gift', 'Satin Gift' and, best of all, 'Santa's Gift'. One wishes nurseries would understand that it is fine to reject a plant because of ethical issues with the name, but it is not acceptable to rename it willy-nilly.

RHODODENDRON 'SATAN'S GIFT' planted beside the *Schefflera septulosa*   ABBIE JURY

RHODODENDRON 'BUTTERMAID'

ABBIE JURY

Felix was very taken with the big, scented blooms of *R. konori*, and his own hybrids were the pink *R.* 'Cherry Pie', red *R.* 'Hot Gossip' – both sister seedlings of a *R. viriosum* hybrid crossed with *R. konori* – and *R.* 'Lipstick'. *R.* 'Cherry Pie' is particularly lush and has good bushy, spreading growth along with a good flower (though much of the scent has gone) and we still rate it as a good garden plant.

R. 'Red Rover' (*viriosum* x *javanicum*) is another of Felix's early hybrids that we continue to rate for its bushy growth habit, healthy characteristics and plenty of good red flowers in a mid-size. However his *R. jasminiflorum* hybrid called *R.* 'Lullaby' has dropped off the radar now and, while a good performer, *R.* 'Lulu' (unknown) has probably been superseded by modern selections with more flowers to the truss.

By the time Mark started hybridising vireyas, there was a veritable explosion of recently discovered and newly imported species becoming available. He collected every single one he could lay his hands on at the time and propagated a few to distribute to collectors. Our nursery records show that we produced over 60 different species at that time, and very

RHODODENDRON 'SWEET CHERRY'   ABBIE JURY

difficult most of them were too. The death rate in the species was far higher than in the hybrids, both in the nursery and when planted in the garden. It was with some relief that we decided after a few years that the few collectors in the country (there were probably only five or ten of them) had everything we held so we stopped feeling obliged to produce them. Similarly, we decided that it was not critical to keep every species represented in the garden. We have never coveted a national collection of any plant genus because we would prefer to garden with plants which justify their position as being garden worthy. Only some of the vireya species perform well for us – we would be sorry to lose varieties such as *R. himantodes*, *R. goodenoughii*, *R. taxifolium*, *R. hellwigii*, *R. macgregoriae* and *R. konori* but many of the other species are either too difficult for us to keep going, or not worth the effort (*R. inconspicuum*, we have always felt, was particularly well named).

So Mark had a much bigger plant palette to work with and this included an ever increasing number of new hybrids as well as the species. Vireyas were suddenly a fashion plant in New Zealand; they were seen as a wonderful alternative for warmer areas of the country where the hardy rhododendrons do not thrive. Added to that, in a country where we would like

RHODODENDRON 'CHERRY PIE'   ABBIE JURY

to be tropical but aren't, vireyas fitted that exotic look and often obliged by flowering throughout the year. From being an unknown plant family with no market at all, they were a gardening sensation for a few years in the nineties.

Fashions change and vireyas are no longer as popular as they were – they are somewhat harder to keep alive, let alone looking good, than many people realised – but in those heady days, there was an insatiable demand for new varieties which had large luscious blooms with heady fragrance and large, heavily felted foliage. Unfortunately, this sometimes meant using breeder parents which, with the passage of time, have not proven to be particularly resilient in our climate.

Mark was also keen to extend the flower form of vireyas into full trusses which more closely resemble the hardy rhododendrons. Many of the species and early hybrids are quite sparse in their flowering and have few flowers to the truss. He also wanted to explore what could be done with colour.

With the benefit of 20 years' experience, he has gone full circle and come back to the point his father reached earlier – a conclusion that it is more important to produce healthy plants which stay alive, with compact growth and masses of flowers as top priorities. More

hardiness and less 'flash and dash', one could say. This tends to mean sacrificing individual bloom size, foliage size and often fragrance. It may end up that his *R. macgregoriae* hybrid, *R.* 'Mango Sunset', proves to be one of his best. While he achieved the much fuller truss he was looking for, it is just a good all round performer without being spectacular.

Market demands meant Mark made the same mistakes as many other vireya breeders – selecting new cultivars on the beauty of their blooms and on initial performance as a nursery plant. The test of longevity rests, for us, on long term health and performance as a garden plant. More than we would wish have fallen by the wayside. *R.* 'Candy Sunrise' (*konori* x Halo series) had beautiful, big fragrant flowers with good colour but was very susceptible to *Phytophthora*. Ditto the red *R.* 'Sweet Cherry' (*konori* x *hellwigii*) – wonderful as a garden plant but not easy in the nursery, R. 'Strawberry Fields' (Satan's Gift x *brookeanum*) – gorgeous big red flower but leggy growth over time and inclined to die, *R.* 'Orange Sparkles' (*retusum* x *macgregoriae*) and cute little *R.* 'Jellybean' (Red Rover x *stenophyllum*).

R. 'Frosted Candy', another of the *konori* x Halo series hybrids, is performing very well as a large garden plant (now two metres plus which

RHODODENDRON 'MANGO SUNSET'

ABBIE JURY

RHODODENDRON 'JAFFA'   ABBIE JURY

is large for a vireya) and it has huge blooms, but again is difficult in the nursery with an unacceptably high death rate from *Phytophthora*.

R. 'Jaffa' (Halo series x *javanicum*) is in the right direction for a full truss; there are now up to 15 large blooms per flower head (which is a big increase from the two to five range of many of the species and early hybrids) and a good strong orange combined with large lettuce green foliage. It is more frost tender and sensitive than the tougher cultivars (which tend to be those with R. *macgregoriae*, R. *viriosum* or R. *saxifragoides* in their parentage). It certainly has the right tropical look and is a better nursery plant than many.

R. 'Pink Jazz' (*konori* x Halo series) is another splendid large grower with enormous blooms – bright pink with a central star of cream and scented too. It also has the stand-out feature of deep maroon new growth and even the old foliage keeps the burgundy tint. It is not easy as a nursery plant and it is too big for many gardens, but the plants we have in our garden are standing the test of time. We have a special fondness for this one. Mark rarely names plants after people, but this one is for our older daughter who, in her teens, was called Jazz by many friends and who nursed a penchant for wearing hot pink.

Mark has always been lukewarm about R. 'Peach Puff' ([*phaeopeplum* x *leucogigas*] x

viriosum selfed) because he regards the pastel peach colouring as insipid. It was an interior fashion colour a decade ago and I still find it very pretty. Again the truss is satisfyingly full with big blooms, good scent and felted foliage.

Of that type of larger flowered, scented hybrid, R. 'Sweet Vanilla' ([*leucogigas* x *viriosum*] x Silken Shimmer) is probably the best garden plant for fragrance. Its flowers, while not huge, are a good size, opening soft pink and fading out to cream. This is one plant which garden visitors regularly ask about when in flower – always a good indicator of showy performance. R. 'Sherbet Rose' (Hot Gossip sister x *herzogii*) matches R. 'Sweet Vanilla' for scent and it is very floriferous but the small tubular mid-pink blooms simply aren't showy enough for most people. We still like it because we don't want only big showy or blowsy vireyas in the garden, but we stopped producing it commercially because scent alone was not enough to sell the plant.

PRACTICAL MATTERS

Vireya rhododendrons must rank amongst the easiest of the woody plants to propagate but one of the hardest to produce commercially. Neither are they bulletproof as garden plants. As long as you have firm, green material, it is easy to get cuttings to root. You don't even need rooting hormone. In fact it is so easy that we routinely showed customers how to take autumn cuttings so they could have back up plants lest their specimen get taken out by a hard frost or wet roots. The one critical issue is to remember to have a generous sized cutting

RHODODENDRON 'PINK JAZZ'   ABBIE JURY

RHODODENDRON
'SWEET VANILLA'

ABBIE JURY

and to take the sliver off two sides of the stem (wounding). Vireyas put their roots out from the exposed cambium layer and having two wounds gives a more balanced root system and therefore more stability.

It is keeping them alive after rooting which is the tricky part, especially in nursery production. Vireyas are not only frost tender and deeply intolerant of wet feet (sodden root systems), but they are vulnerable to pretty much every strain of *Phytophthora* and a fair range of other diseases common in nursery production.

In the wild, many of the vireya species are epiphytic or semi epiphytic which is an indicator that their roots need open conditions. This is what fits them to a role as permanent pot plants though they appear to last better in pots which are more permeable (terracotta or wood) than in containers which are impermeable (glazed pottery or plastic) and dependent for drainage on one or two holes in the bottom.

When producing commercial runs of vireyas, we maintained a rigorous spray programme to keep disease at bay. Even so, we tolerated a far higher mortality rate in nursery plants than we would in any other crop. We have always produced them outdoors, under protective shade cloth and overhead irrigation – identical conditions to most of our nursery crops.

CORRECTLY PREPARED VIREYA CUTTINGS

ABBIE JURY

Vireyas tend to put on a lot of top growth, supported by small, inadequate root systems (an indicator of their epiphytic origins), and new growth is often very soft and brittle. As nursery crops in our climate, they grow very rapidly at all times of the year and it is possible to get a saleable plant through in half the time of a hardy rhododendron, but they are correspondingly more vulnerable to damage by mishandling and disease.

We are blessed with a climate which enables us to use vireya rhododendrons as garden plants. We are not entirely frost free so we use them on the woodland margins where temperatures

VIREYAS PLANTED IN A GARDEN BORDER   ABBIE JURY

may get cool but never cold enough to cause significant damage. Any frost at all can burn the most tender varieties which includes anything with *R. leucogigas*, *R. konori*, *R. hellwigii* and sometimes even *R. laetum* in the breeding. The hardier types will take two or three degrees of frost without damage but more than that can be a problem. Get it up to five degrees of frost and plants can be killed stone dead. The beauty of vireyas as garden plants is that they

do not have a set flowering season so if you have sufficient numbers, there are always plants in bloom – even in the depths of winter. Added to that, they are tolerant of hard pruning so easy to renovate. Even when cut back to bare wood, most will force out dormant leaf buds from old wood and can be bushy and fresh again within a matter of months, even if it takes longer for them to set flower buds. It is a misconception that vireyas are all tropical plants. While natural habitats are often in the tropical latitudes, they are in elevated sites which cool the temperatures.

With their climatic limitations, vireya rhododendrons will never have the geographic distribution of hardier plants and, no matter how good the hybrids, they are unlikely to achieve international standing. There is a long way to go yet in breeding reliable cultivars which are likely to stand the test of time but it is certainly interesting to have been in from the early days on the development of new selections and Mark will continue to work with them here, albeit on a rather casual basis.

PROMISING LEMON SEEDLING
– the breeding continues   ABBIE JURY

Abbie Jury

is a garden writer who gardens at Tikorangi, The Jury Garden, in New Zealand with her husband Mark Jury

Expanding the palette: new frontiers in magnolia hybridisation

DENNIS LEDVINA

MAGNOLIA **'SUNSET SWIRL'** displays its fabulous glowing colours and perfect pinwheel form

DENNIS LEDVINA

ON MY VISITS TO THE WEST COAST of the US, I was always impressed with the early blooming magnolias of sub-genus *Yulania* with their gorgeous display of precocious flowers in early spring. These included *Magnolia campbellii, M. sargentiana, M. sprengeri* and, of course, the well-known *M. denudata*. Most of the US and parts of Europe, that have a continental climate, experience freezes that badly damage these early bloomers. Hybridising the early bloomers in sub-genus *Yulania* with some of the later

bloomers in the sub-genus such as *M. liliiflora* and *M. acuminata* can resolve that problem. We are all familiar with *M.* x *soulangeana*, a cross of *M. liliiflora* x *M. denudata* that was made over 100 years ago. These include noted cultivars such as *M.* 'Lennei', *M.* 'Brozzonii', *M.* 'Alexandrina', and others more recently selected.

The Brooklyn Botanic Garden was a pioneer in magnolia hybridising with their original crosses of *M. acuminata* x *M. denudata* resulting

MAGNOLIA 'ROSE MARIE'   DENNIS LEDVINA

in the well-known cultivar *M.* 'Elizabeth', as well as the lesser known *M.* x *brooklynensis* 'Evamaria' , a cross of *M. acuminata* x *M. liliiflora*. Later releases by the Brooklyn Botanic Garden include *M.* 'Yellow Bird', *M.* 'Lois', *M.* 'Judy Zuk', and *M.* 'Hattie Carthan'. Joe McDaniel, of the University of Illinois, also crossed *M. acuminata* with *M. liliiflora* which resulted in the well-known cultivar *M.* 'Woodsman'.

My work in hybridising began when I met two great mentors, Phil Savage in Michigan, and Augie Kehr in North Carolina. Both Phil and Augie were very helpful in providing me with scions and pollen of many of their primary crosses which provided the genetic groundwork for much of my work. Phil crossed *M. acuminata* with *M. denudata* which resulted in his famous *M.* 'Butterflies'. He also made the primary crosses of *M. acuminata* x *M. campbellii*, *M. acuminata* x *M. sargentiana* var. *robusta*, *M. acuminata* x *M. sprengeri* 'Diva', and *M. acuminata* x various *M.* x *soulangeana* cultivars. These hybrids provided the genetic material for many of my future crosses. Augie also made many of these primary crosses as well as his famous *M.* 'Daybreak', a cross of *M.* 'Woodsman' with *M.*

'Tina Durio', and was also involved in doubling the chromosome count of several magnolias including the famous *M.* 'Gold Cup', an octoploid with thick tepals that maintain an upright form.

Having this vast genetic pool available to me, I began my work with three primary goals in mind when hybridising in sub-genus *Yulania*:

• Develop later blooming magnolias that will not be harmed by late spring frosts.
• Develop magnolias that will be hardy in a USDA Zone 4–5 (able to withstand minimum temperatures colder than –26°C and therefore suitable for almost all of Europe).
• Extend the blooming period of magnolias.

Using late blooming *M. acuminata* and *M. liliiflora* in sub-genus *Yulania* can achieve the first and second goals, but they also pose disadvantages that need to be overcome. *M. acuminata* has small greenish yellow flowers that tend to be hidden by its leaves and can bring a dull brown color to the resulting hybrids. The deep purple color of *M. liliiflora* can dominate the delicate pink of some of the species in the subgenus. While crossing the two generally will result in a muddy purple flower like *M.* 'Woodsman' or a yellow flower like *M.* 'Yellow Bird', both can produce excellent hybrids in the succeeding generation. This is well illustrated in *M.* 'Daybreak', where *M.* 'Woodsman' is the seed parent, and in *M.* 'Blushing Belle', where *M.* 'Yellow Bird' is the seed parent. Other hybrids that are at least one half *M. acuminata* that have been excellent seed parents are *M.* 'Red Baron', *M.* 'Black Beauty', and *M.* 'Yellow Lantern'. *M.* 'Black Beauty' x *M.* 'Gorgeous' is producing some attractive looking plants with reddish-bronze new growth.

It may be difficult to develop a magnolia that will bloom the entire summer, but *M. liliiflora* and *M. acuminata,* in addition to adding hardiness, also have an extended blooming period. *M. liliiflora* hybrids such as *M.* 'March to Frost', *M.* 'Ann', *M.* 'Betty', *M.* 'Jane' can be late summer repeat bloomers if enhanced by sufficient rainfall. These need to be crossed with *M.* 'Yellow Bird', which is another repeat bloomer. Some of the New Zealand hybrids like *M.* 'Genie' and *M.* 'Cleopatra' also can be repeat bloomers so crossing them with *M.* 'Yellow

MAGNOLIA 'BLUSHING BELLE'

DENNIS LEDVINA

Bird' could produce a long blooming magnolia with a good purple color. While *M.* 'Daybreak' and *M.* 'Rose Marie' will have a spring bloom of about a month, there generally is no repeat bloom on them but it may be possible to extend their spring bloom for an additional month by crossing them with some of the New Zealand hybrids.

Although hardiness is my prime objective, a secondary goal is to develop narrowly fastigiate trees that will accommodate a compact landscape. Hybrids with a narrow growth habit include *M.* 'March to Frost', *M.* 'Sunsprite', *M.* 'Sunspire', *M.* 'Black Beauty', and *M.* 'Daybreak'. I have made several crosses utilising these hybrids, but it is too early to determine what the ultimate size of the resulting hybrids will be. Making crosses with some of the smaller-growing New Zealand hybrids like *M.* 'Genie' could also accomplish these goals. My most promising narrow growing hybrid thus far is a cross of *M.* 'Yellow Bird' with *M.* 'Apollo' with burgundy-red flowers. It bloomed as a young seedling, has many lateral flower buds characteristic of *M.* 'Yellow Bird', and an extending blooming period.

Another secondary goal is to develop a multi-tepalled magnolia with a good red/pink color. Crosses of *M.* x *loebneri*

MAGNOLIA 'BURGUNDY SPIRE'   DENNIS LEDVINA

TOP ROW: MAGNOLIA 'CRESCENDO'*, MAGNOLIA* 'ROSEANNE'
MIDDLE ROW: MAGNOLIA 'ANGELICA'*, MAGNOLIA* 'PINK DELIGHT'
BOTTOM ROW: MAGNOLIA 'COTTON CANDY'*, MAGNOLIA* 'ROYAL SPLENDOR'

DENNIS LEDVINA

'Leonard Messel' with M. x *loebneri* 'White Rose' have resulted in flowers with up to 24 tepals, but are a soft lavender-pink color. Quite likely there would not be enough pigmentation if the crosses are made within the species. If a cross of a diploid with a large number of tepals like M. × *loebneri* 'White Rose', M. × *loebneri* 'Encore' or the product of its self-cross, M. *stellata* 'Pink Perfection', or M. × *loebneri* 'Wildcat' were made with pollen of a red-colored magnolia like M. 'Black Tulip', M. 'Cleopatra', or M. 'Genie', the resulting hybrid may have good red/pink pigmentation, but the dominance of the pollen parent with its higher chromosome count may not substantially increase the number of tepals. Backcrossing the resulting hybrids to the M. × *loebneri* selections may be necessary to increase the number of tepals.

The following are some of the named selections I have introduced:

M. **'Rose Marie'**, which is a cross of M. 'Pink Surprise' × M. 'Daybreak', is one quarter M. *acuminata* and one quarter M. *liliiflora* and is very late blooming. M. 'Rose Marie' starts blooming 1–2 weeks later than M. x *soulangeana* and can bloom for as long as a month; it and M. 'Daybreak' are my longest blooming magnolias in sub-genus *Yulania*. M. 'Rose Marie' also has a nice columnar grow habit similar to M. 'Daybreak', a characteristic that is very desirable to landscapers. M. 'Rose Marie' is very seed fertile and has been crossed with some of the New Zealand hybrids such as M. 'Genie', M. 'Cleopatra', M. 'Felix Jury', and M. 'Ian's Red' with the goal of developing a hardy magnolia with the color intensity of M. *campbellii* 'Lanarth'. Both M. 'Rose Marie' and M. 'Daybreak' also have been crossed with M. 'Gold Cup' with the goal of maintaining their vivid pink color and obtaining the flower form of M. 'Gold Cup', which has very thick, upright tepals.

M. **'Pink Charm'** is a sister seedling of M. 'Rose Marie' with similar color but with a more lily formed flower. The tree is very fastigiate and has a long blooming period similar to M. 'Rose Marie'.

M. **'Blushing Belle'**, a cross of M. 'Yellow Bird' x M. 'Caerhays Belle' has gorgeous pink flowers similar to M. 'Caerhays Belle', but with a bit less salmon color than its pollen parent. The deep pink exterior and lighter pink interior show no traces of yellow. It is much hardier than M. 'Caerhays Belle' and has bloomed after −30°C. It also blooms later than M. 'Caerhays Belle' and thus avoids late spring frosts. The flowers are a bit smaller than M. 'Caerhays Belle', but maintain a better upright form. M. 'Blushing Belle' is seed sterile, but has good pollen fertility and has been crossed with M. 'Rose Marie', M. 'Red Baron' (M. *acuminata* x M. 'Big Dude') and others.

M. **'Crescendo'** is a cross of M. 'Yellow Lantern' x M. 'Big Dude' (M. 'Yellow Lantern' is a cross of M. *acuminata* var. *subcordata* x M. x *soulangeana* 'Alexandrina' and M. 'Big Dude' is a cross of M. *sprengeri* 'Diva' x M. 'Picture'). Huge pink flowers emerge from tiny flower buds to create a 'crescendo' effect. M. 'Crescendo' is a very free flowering, long blooming magnolia that was completely hardy at −30°C.

M. **'Roseanne'** is a cross of M. *liliiflora* 'O'Neill' x M. *kobus* 'Norman Gould'. This hybrid has six or seven tepals which are rich lavender pink on the outside and a lighter pink on the inside. The tepals are very broad and retain their upright form. M. 'Roseanne' is a fertile tetraploid that is producing some excellent hybrids. The foliage is semi-glossy with a heavy texture.

M. **'Royal Splendor'** is a cross of M. 'Pink Royalty' x M. 'Daybreak' – M. 'Pink Royalty' being a cross of M. *acuminata* x M. 'Dark Diva'. The exterior of the nine pointed tepals is an intense reddish pink, the interior being a lighter pink. This hybrid bloomed as a six foot seedling and continues to be very floriferous with many lateral flower buds which prolong the bloom for as long as a month. This is the most intensely colored magnolia in my collection that glows like a beacon in the distance.

M. **'Sunset Swirl'** is a cross of M. 'Pink Royalty' x M. 'Daybreak'. A pink flowered magnolia that displays the gorgeous colors of a brilliant sunset. While the color is similar to that of M. 'Daybreak', the advantage of this magnolia is its excellent flower form which matures to a flat, pinwheel form with no floppiness.

M. **'Cotton Candy'** is a cross of M. 'Red Baron' x M. 'Blushing Belle'. The huge flowers have nine broad tepals that are a medium pink on both the exterior and the interior and show no

*TOP ROW: **MAGNOLIA** 'ANGEL MIST', **MAGNOLIA** 'ORIENTAL CHARM'*
*MIDDLE ROW: **MAGNOLIA** 'SILK ROAD', **MAGNOLIA** 'EXOTIC STAR'*
*BOTTOM ROW: **MAGNOLIA** 'SIMPLE PLEASURES', **MAGNOLIA** 'IVORY JEWEL'*

DENNIS LEDVINA

THE SUMPTUOUS BLOOMS OF *MAGNOLIA* 'GOLDEN RAIN'

DENNIS LEDVINA

traces of green or purple. With its genetic background being seven-sixteenths *M. acuminata*, it is a very hardy *'campbellii* type' magnolia for colder climates.

M. '**Burgundy Spire**' is a cross of *M.* 'Yellow Bird' x *M.* 'Apollo'. I was impressed with its very narrow growth habit as a young seedling and thrilled to see it bloom with a clear burgundy exterior and a cream interior. The nine tepals remain upright and do not flop as the flowers age. Because of its abundance of lateral flower buds, it remains in bloom for several weeks. This is a very desirable magnolia for limited garden space.

M. '**Angelica**' is a cross of *M.* 'Pegasus' x *M.* x *soulangeana* 'Sawada's Pink'. It has nine round, cup-shaped tepals that measure over three inches in diameter. The color is a pure white and the flower retains its bowl shape and does not flop with age. *M.* 'Angelica' will develop into a medium sized tree with a bloom time intermediate between *M. cylindrica* and *M.* x *soulangeana*. The seed of this hybrid was collected from the original cross made by Phil Savage. Good seed fertility.

M. '**Pink Delight**' is a cross of *M.* 'Alexandrina' x *M.* 'Galaxy'. This magnolia has extremely fragrant, very wide tepalled, flowers of a high-quality lavender-pink. Extremely good seed fertility.

M. '**Angel Mist**' is a cross of *M. officinalis* x *M.* x *wieseneri* grown from open pollinated seed received from Augie Kehr. The very fragrant, creamy-white flowers have twelve tepals that maintain excellent form. Moderate seed fertility.

M. '**Oriental Charm**' is a cross of *M. officinalis* x *M. obovata* and is an extremely fragrant and vigorous grower. The tree is over 40 feet tall and has a trunk diameter of over a foot. The creamy white flowers open in late afternoon and are fragrant throughout the entire yard. Moderate seed fertility.

M. '**Silk Road**' is a cross of *M. tripetala* x (*M. tripetala* x *M. obovata*) with the pleasant fragrance of *M. obovata* and the hardiness of *M. tripetala*. A white, moderately fragrant flower that has slightly narrower tepals than some of the other Rytidospermum hybrids. Excellent seed fertility.

M. **'Sweet Love'** is a cross of *M. sieboldii* x *M.* 'Oriental Charm' – a large white flowered magnolia with up to twelve broad tepals. A fastigiate growing small tree with large tropical looking leaves. This magnolia is very easy to root from softwood cuttings.

M. **'Exotic Star'** is a cross of *M. sieboldii* x *M. grandiflora* 'Russet' which bloomed as a three foot seedling and has been quite floriferous since. The flowers are similar to *M. grandiflora*, but have orange/red stamens. The plant remains evergreen and has rust colored indumentum. Hardiness remains to be tested.

M. **'Simple Pleasures'** is a cross of *M. liliflora* x *M.* 'Norman Gould'. It blooms at a young age with light lavender-pink, cup shaped, slightly fragrant flowers. It flowers in mid-season and is extremely flower bud hardy. A tetraploid hybrid that produces an abundance of seed.

M. **'First Love'** is a cross of *M. liliflora* x *M.* 'Woodsman' and has purple flowers similar to *M. liliflora*, but with greater hardiness. This magnolia has been excellent for further hybridising.

M. **'Wedding Vows'** is a cross of *M.* 'Woodsman' x '*M.* 'Big Dude' with refined and graceful large ivory-white blossoms that are uniquely interesting. The tepals are long and gently trail like a wedding dress train. Growth habit is fastigiate.

M. **'Ivory Jewel'** is another *M.* 'Woodsman' x '*M.* 'Big Dude' cross. Nine large tepals with a creamy yellow interior and a blush pink exterior grace

MAGNOLIA 'WEDDING VOWS'

DENNIS LEDVINA

this magnolia. A vigorous, hardy tree with a fastigiate growth habit.

M. **'Golden Rain'** is a tetraploid cross of *M. acuminata* x *M.* 'Norman Gould' and has medium yellow flowers with six, very wide, cup-shaped tepals, that cascade downward. This vigorous, tall growing magnolia has shown tremendous hardiness. New foliage emerging in spring is an attractive bronze. Good seed fertility.

M. **'Red Baron'** is a cross of *M. acuminata* x *M.* 'Big Dude'. The flowers are smaller than *M.* 'Big Dude', with a deeper red color and it is much hardier. Excellent seed fertility.

M. SIEBOLDII 'COLOSSUS' × M. INSIGNIS (RED FORM)
unnamed seedling   DENNIS LEDVINA

PART OF THE COLLECTION OF MAGNOLIA HYBRIDS CURRENTLY UNDER ASSESSMENT IN THE GARDEN
DENNIS LEDVINA

A NEW DIRECTION

I am also doing extensive hybridising in sub-genus Magnolia by crossing *M. grandiflora*, *M. virginiana*, *M. tripetala*, *M. obovata*, and *M. sieboldii* with red/pink flowering magnolias from Section *Manglietia* with the goal of developing red/pink flowers in these species.

M. sieboldii 'Colossus' × M. insignis (red form) is, as yet, unnamed. From seed planted in the spring of 2009, this magnolia bloomed in September of 2010. The flower has the rich dark stamens in the center, typical of the Oyama magnolias, as well as a very nice fragrance. The flower has many tepals that almost make it look like a sacred, delicate pink, lotus flower. The attractive foliage has a glossy texture.

CONCLUSION

In conclusion, much work needs to be done and I am happy to see other magnolia enthusiasts becoming actively involved in magnolia hybridising. However, we must be aware that crossing two outstanding cultivars will not always result in a hybrid with the best attributes of both parents, and many disappointing hybrids can result.

Currently I have nearly a thousand hybrids planted out for future evaluation and have been sharing seed with friends throughout the world with the hope that many outstanding cultivars will be introduced in the future.

Dennis Ledvina

has been hybridising magnolias in his Green Bay, Wisconsin garden since the 1970s. A hybridiser of international renown, he is well known for his generosity with scions and seed. He is currently helping to create one of the most extensive collections of Magnolia in the US

Camellias in Brittany

BEE ROBSON

CHANCE BROUGHT US TO BRITTANY. In August 2009 an advertisement appeared in the local paper in Cornwall – *Large country house with grounds wanted to rent for two years.*

We left England in November; a month in the sun with our daughter in New Zealand helped us to recover from the inevitable rigours of preparing the house and garden for occupation by an experimental dementia care project, and the beginning of January witnessed our arrival in a snow-bound France, the car stuffed with essentials – a large French/English dictionary, an oyster knife and my books. We had decided to spend four precious months of our grey nomad gap years in Brittany, with three specific objectives: to learn to speak French, to indulge unstintingly in some of the best seafood in the world and

KNIGHT'S NEW CARNATION WARATAH from Curtis's *Botanical Magazine* (Vol 52 Plate 2577)

CAMELLIA JAPONICA 'PAEONIFLORA ROSEA', from the Chandler & Booth catalogue of 1831 (Illustrations and descriptions of the plants which compose the natural order *Camellieae*)

to pursue my study of 19th century camellia varieties, an interest that was born during the years that I had spent working at the Lost Gardens of Heligan.

At Heligan, as in most of the old gardens in Cornwall, many of the ancient camellias remain unnamed. During the past years, I have developed a method of working to try to identify these old plants. First is to research the garden site to try to establish a planting date.

Second is to record details of the plant itself, the flowers of course, but also the leaves. Flowers can vary enormously, influenced by soil, climatic conditions and by the propensity of camellias to produce flowers of different forms on the same plant. Leaves vary much less: the differences between the leaves of different varieties are subtler than the differences between the flowers but the leaves of different plants of the same variety are unmistakably similar.

The third step is to establish a list of possibilities. To do this I am compiling a list of all of the camellias that were on sale in the UK, from their first appearance in British nursery catalogues dating from the 1820s, to the end of the 19th century, a list sub-divided into colours and forms. This then allows me to come up with a group of varieties stocked by British nurseries that fit the general description of the plant being studied, for example, all the pink formal double camellias with white stripes.

Most nursery catalogues, for example those of James Veitch & Sons or William Rollisson & Sons, give only a very brief description of the listed camellias but there are other contemporaneous publications that contain much more: they include not only detailed descriptions but also illustrations, illustrations that are remarkably accurate both in detail and, more surprisingly, in colour.

William Curtis started the *Botanical Magazine* in 1787 and by the 1820s details of some of the earliest English camellias began to appear.

In this same period, one of the early English nurseries, that of Chandler & Buckingham, published its own illustrated catalogue in 1825. This was followed by the Chandler & Booth catalogues of 1831 and 1837, with illustrations by Alfred Chandler and descriptions by the first acknowledged camellia expert, William Beattie Booth.

On the Continent there was huge enthusiasm for camellia breeding. In Belgium, the first of the Verschaffelt nursery catalogues, *Nouvelle Iconographie des Camellias,* was published in 1848, while during the same period in France, M. L'Abbé Berlèse produced his great work, *Iconographie du Genre Camellia*, three volumes that contain the exquisite and astonishingly accurate illustrations of M. J-J. Jung.

These publications, together with others from Germany and Italy, contain descriptions and illustrations of many hundreds of camellias and therefore, within their pages, are illustrations of most of the camellias that were available from British nurseries during the 19th century.

Camellia Ignea ou Ignivoma

CAMELLIA IGNEA OU IGNIVOMA from Berlèse's *Iconographie du Genre Camellia* 1841 (Vol 1)

Identifying camellias from such illustrations and descriptions is by no means foolproof; there are many pitfalls, but certainly, when studying old and unnamed camellias, the method gives a good starting point.

Confident identification can only come from comparison with living plants of trustworthy provenance and it was for this reason that I came to Brittany.

It was New Year, we arrived in a blizzard, the main roads were all but impassable and there were camellias blooming. Cornwall and Brittany are so very similar: the rugged coastlines with crashing waves, their shared Celtic history, saints and place names: the Breton name for Cornwall – Cornouaille - is also the name of one of the areas of coastal Brittany. Cornwall has many camellias but in Brittany they are a way of life.

There are many places to look at camellias: they are in every garden, they decorate roundabouts, line the middle of dual

OLD CAMELLIA CLOSE TO THE CATHEDRAL SAINT- CORENTIN, identified by Pascal Vieu as *C. JAPONICA* **'MADAME PEPIN'**   BEE ROBSON

carriageways: they are planted around churches, in cemeteries, in car parks, outside municipal offices. Many of these are modern cultivars, bred for their colour, flamboyance and hardiness but the tradition of using camellias in this way is not new.

In Quimper, for example, there is a magnificent *Camellia japonica* 'Madame Pepin' by the river close to the Cathedral.

Further east, towards the city of Nantes, flourishes one of the oldest camellias on record in Brittany, the venerable *C. japonica* 'Latifolia', growing in the cemetery at La Trinité sur Mer.

My mission, however, was to find varieties that have an irreproachable provenance, and with this in mind, there were two places I wanted to visit.

The first was the Domaine of Trevarez. I had met curator Pascal Vieu at the recent ICS congress in Falmouth and it was at his invitation that we

drove north towards Châteauneuf de Faou, to the fairytale pink château perched on the hillside outside the little town.

James de Kerjegu commissioned the château and its construction, begun in 1893, took ten years. It is built of a curious pink brick, which glows in the sunlight. It has had a chequered history. Requisitioned by the German army of occupation in 1941, it was badly damaged by bombing raids in 1944. We asked who had committed such an outrage and were told by Pascal – 'You did!'

The château stands high on a ridge: to the east, planted woodland; to the west, a formal pond with great stone fountains and a curving sweep of stone steps that leads to a rocky gorge; to the north the views are spectacular across the valley and immediately in front of the château are formal gardens, the intricate design edged with box and accentuated by statuary.

A great semi-circle encloses these formal gardens and it is here that the oldest camellias at Trevarez are to be found.

There are 27 ancient camellias, then heavy with blooms, a few of them named but, as is so often the case with old camellia collections, many of these plants remain unidentified. So, glorious as they are, my real interest lay in the collection of new plants of old camellia varieties.

CAMELLIA JAPONICA **'LATIFOLIA'** in the cemetery at La Trinité sur Mer
BEE ROBSON

ANCIENT CAMELLIAS in the formal gardens in front of the Château de Tevarez   BEE ROBSON

Pascal Vieu, Collections Curator at Trevarez, takes great care when introducing young plants into the collection to ensure that each has an excellent provenance. It is therefore possible to rely on these camellias as benchmarks by which to identify others and so I was able to make many additions to my database including a fine example of *C. japonica* 'Marguerita Coleoni'.

The second place on my list to visit was Les Jardins des Plantes, next to the railway station in Nantes.

This is no private garden, no moneyed estate; this is a public botanical garden. It began as an apothecaries' garden in 1626 and was greatly benefited in 1726 by a royal decree from Louis XV instructing the masters of ships to bring seeds and plants from foreign lands to the Garden of Medicinal Plants.

There is a statue of Jean-Marie Ecorchard who became director of Les Jardins in 1840 and who laid the foundations for the botanical garden as it is today.

There are more than six hundred varieties of camellias in Les Jardins des Plantes. Many of the old varieties are planted in borders that

follow the sweeping curve of the path from the entrance close to the railway station up to the main entrance gates. Across the centre of the garden is a broad avenue, studded at

CAMELLIA JAPONICA 'MADAME AMBROISE VERSCHAFFELT', Les Jardins des Plantes, Nantes
BEE ROBSON

SIMILAR VARIETIES AT LES JARDINS DES PLANTES demonstrate the difficulty of identification by flower alone
TOP ROW: CAMELLIA JAPONICA 'PICTURATA', *C. JAPONICA* 'MARGUERITE GOUILLON'
BOTTOM ROW: C. JAPONICA 'GENERAL LAMORICIÈRE', *C. JAPONICA* 'COLVILLII'   BEE ROBSON

intervals by old camellias, that leads to another area of more recent planting, a mixture of old varieties and younger introductions. What makes this botanical garden such a joy, and so immensely rewarding to work in, is that all these camellias are clearly and, for the most part, accessibly labelled.

For any camellia lover, visiting Les Jardins des Plantes in March is like being a child in a sweet shop! There were varieties I had long wished to see, among them was *C. japonica* 'Madame Ambroise Verschaffelt', featured in the Veitch catalogue of 1868.

Here too was *C. japonica* 'Anna Bruneau', one of the camellias that appears in the Gill catalogues of the 1920s. Richard Gill was for many years Head Gardener at the Shilson estate at Tremough near Falmouth and who, after the estate was sold, established his own nursery in the grounds at Tremough. Richard Gill is best known for his beautiful and distinctive hybrids developed using the Indian rhododendrons obtained from Sir William Hooker at Kew in the 1860s, but, amongst the many other plants raised in his nursery, there were 15 camellia varieties. *C. japonica* 'Anna Bruneau' was one of these. I have not yet found it at Tremough, but, even if no longer there, it should be in other Cornish gardens, supplied originally by Richard Gill.

Here in Les Jardins des Plantes was the opportunity to distinguish between such varieties as *C. japonica* 'Picturata', *C. japonica* 'Marguerite Gouillon', *C. japonica* 'General Lamoricière' and *C. japonica* 'Colvillii'.

Superficially, the flower forms are similar and so the accurate recording of the leaves becomes of paramount importance, a conviction shared by both Pascal Vieu and René Malhaus, former president of the Société Bretonne du Camellia, who together are developing a system of leaf classification. With a little practice, a microwave oven provides a quick and convenient way of drying leaves for preservation.

The reputation of Les Jardins des Plantes for the accuracy of its nomenclature owes much to the nurseries in Brittany: it is through the longevity and the integrity of these nurseries that so many of these ancient varieties have been preserved.

CAMELLIA JAPONICA 'ANNA BRUNEAU',
Les Jardins des Plantes, Nantes   BEE ROBSON

CAMELLIA JAPONICA 'EDIT DE NANTES',
(Thoby Nursery, 2003) seen in the garden of
Alfred Lemaître   BEE ROBSON

Historically, the most famous nursery was that of Henri Guichard, established in 1864. Henri was succeeded by his son, who in turn was succeeded by his sisters, the Guichard Soeurs. *C. japonica* 'Souvenir de Henri Guichard' 1908 (syn 'Hikarugenji') commemorates this dynasty.

One of the Guichard nursery sites, at Carquefou, was taken over in 1911 by Claude Thoby and then later by Alfred Lemaître. Alfred spent many years in charge of propagation at the Thoby nursery, raising new varieties such as *C. japonica* 'Edit de Nantes'.

It is due to this continuity of dedicated nurserymen that the nomenclature is so reliable. The Lemaître nursery is now run by Alfred's son Joël, but Alfred and his wife Thérèse continue to dedicate their lives and their garden to the care and preservation of valuable nursery stock; many of the ancient varieties that they have are from the original stock of the Guichard nurseries, and Alfred continues to be horticultural advisor to Les Jardins des Plantes.

Not all nurseries and collections are historic. We were fortunate enough to visit Parc ar Brug close to Guingamp, the home of Fānch and Anne Le Moal. Fānch and Anne share a passion for camellias and have spent more than 35 years developing their remarkable collection.

When we visited, the garden had been ravaged by extreme weather: heavy snow had caused a

A NEW INTRODUCTION FROM FÃNCH LE MOAL:
CAMELLIA HYBRID 'PARC AR BRUG'   BEE ROBSON

provide an agreeable way of studying the vast range of camellias grown in Brittany.

The Société Bretonne du Camellia's annual show in 2010 at Guingamp had some delightful formal displays as well as unusual outdoor exhibits.

It was, however, an exhibit at a little show at Rospico which led to a new discovery.

I had noticed a camellia called 'Scorrier' – an unexpected name in the depths of Brittany.

I photographed it and forgot it, forgot it until this spring when I visited Scorrier House in Cornwall for the first time and photographed a very old single pink. A memory niggled and eventually I tracked it down in the pictures from Rospico.

C. japonica 'Scorrier' was featured in the Treseder nursery catalogue of fifty years ago and is described as being taken from *'An old lost name*

great deal of damage, crushing some plants and smashing others apart, but even so, the extent of the collection was impressive and included many species, many old varieties and also newer ones such as *C. japonica* 'Kick Off', *C. japonica* 'Lipstick' and *C.* x *williamsii* 'Tulip Time'.

An important part of their work is breeding new varieties. Beehives facilitate pollination to produce new seedlings, and promising sports are stabilized. The semi-double hybrid *C.* 'Parc ar Brug', and *C. japonica* 'Ville de Guingamp' are two of many examples of new introductions. Anne and Fãnch also carry on the delightful tradition of naming a new camellia for each addition to their family.

The Société Bretonne du Camellia provides the focus for camellia culture in Brittany and the shows of the SBC and other camellia societies

INDOOR DISPLAY AT GUINGAMP SHOW 2010

BEE ROBSON

OLD VARIETY REDISCOVERED?
LEFT: **CAMELLIA JAPONICA 'SCORRIER'** photographed at the Rospico Camellia Show 2010
RIGHT: **THOUGHT TO BE C. JAPONICA 'SCORRIER'** photographed at Scorrier House in Cornwall 2011

BEE ROBSON

camellia growing on a wall at Scorrier.' (Source: *Treseders Special Camellia List 1964*)

So, an exhibit from a little show in Brittany may possibly have led to another unnamed Cornish camellia being identified!

There is a rich heritage of camellia culture in Brittany and a passion for the old varieties as well as the new. It is this passion for the ancient varieties, and the expert work that is being done to bring these historic plants back into cultivation, that makes Brittany so exciting. Notable amongst these experts are the Lemaîtres for their care of original Guichard material; Pascal Vieu for the development of the collection at Trevarez and for the new work he is doing on leaf classification; Fãnch and Anne Le Moal for their comprehensive collection and their new introductions, and Rene Malhaus for his untiring and enthusiastic pursuit of knowledge, and the careful, methodical way in which he researches new sites, in preparation for the process of identification. This work he shares with Cathie Joly, webmaster of the excellent website lovcam.org, whose beautiful pictures and accurate information are of huge benefit to any camellia lover.

These pictures from Brittany – the flowers of course, but equally importantly, the leaves – will, I hope, enable me to continue the work of trying to put names to some of Cornwall's old camellias, but, to quote from the celebrated Florentine camellia breeder Cesare Franchetti:

'...one flowering is not enough to make a certain judgment of a flower.....'

I will just have to go back!

ACKNOWLEDGEMENTS

All photographs are my copyright. Photographs of plates from Chandler & Buckingham, Chandler & Booth, Curtis's *Botanical Magazine*, Berlèse's *Iconographie du Genre Camellia* and Verschaffelt's *Nouvelle Iconographie des Camellias* are taken from the facsimile books published by Mr Shin'ichiro Kishikawa. I am indebted to Mr Kishikawa for allowing to me to photograph and reproduce these images.

Bee Robson

is an author and camellia expert specialising in the old varieties in Cornish gardens. She was responsible for the initial identification and curation of the collection at the Lost Gardens of Heligan

Weighing in: discovering the ploidy of hybrid elepidote rhododendrons

SALLY PERKINS, JOHN PERKINS, JOSÉ CERCA DE OLIVEIRA, MARIANA CASTRO, SILVIA CASTRO & JOÃO LOUREIRO

TRIPLOID *RHODODENDRON* 'PHYLLIS KORN' is the offspring of a triploid (*R.* 'Gomer Waterer') and parent to a diploid (*R.* 'Summer Peach')

SALLY & JOHN PERKINS

WHEN WE MENTION THE WORD 'PLOIDY' most gardeners' eyes glaze over. What does ploidy have to do with their beautiful garden specimens of rhododendrons?

Yet if we mention *Rhododendron* 'Cynthia', *R.* 'Gomer Waterer', *R.* 'Grace Seabrook', *R.* 'Horizon Monarch', *R.* 'Pink Pearl', *R.* 'Phyllis Korn', *R.* 'Point Defiance', *R.* 'Taurus' or *R.* 'Trude Webster', gardeners quickly add that these are among their favorite rhododendrons or high on their wish list. Yes, these rhododendrons display 'something different' and are 'highly desirable'.

WEIGHING IN

As dozens more rhododendrons with larger than normal ploidy levels are revealed below, we hope that gardeners begin to see the connection with characteristics of thickness in the leaf and firmness in flower substance. Indeed, remarkable vigor and substance overall, coupled with outstanding floral performance at a young age, starts to make sense. Even gardeners, who do not want to talk about ploidy, love talking about polyploids.

We are not geneticists. We do have science backgrounds though, combined with a passion for knowledge. Our ploidy journey began as simple curiosity combined with a willingness to coordinate with others, to scour the rhododendron literature and the web, and do some field work, leading to more discoveries than we ever imagined.

First, when we refer to ploidy we mean the 'size' of the plant's genetic material. In seed bearing plants, the genetic material is found in the cell's nucleus, packed into structures called **chromosomes**.

There are two different techniques used to determine how much genetic material is in a cell and therefore, an estimate of the number of chromosomes that are present in that cell. One can 'count the ways' or 'weigh the counts'.

Count the ways: The classic way to determine the number of chromosomes in a plant is to 'visualize' the chromosomes with stain where they are actively growing, as in a root tip, and then count the different pairs under the microscope. Reports are that this is very tedious (more so in rhododendrons), prone to error, and even eager graduate students are reluctant to co-operate. There are very few studies using this method, those that exist are mostly older, and there is even less duplication of results.

Weigh the counts: With flow cytometry it is possible to weigh the genetic material by taking healthy plant tissue and measuring the weight of the genetic content. This technique is much less time consuming and therefore easier to verify by duplicating results.

Flow cytometry was developed to detect mutations in tumors and cancer cells. If the cells are normal and growing, there would be a small number of cells with double the weight of their chromosomes, as they would be in the phase prior to division. Any cells with less than or more than that weight would be an indication of mutations of the amount of genetic material in the cell (i.e. cancer). This valuable technique can also be used to detect the normal weight of genetic material in different species and hybrids of rhododendrons.

POLYPLOIDY: BEGINNING WITH 1, 2, 3, 4, 5

In most plant cells, i.e. leaves, stems, roots and some parts of the flower, the chromosomes are paired with a matching chromosome to form the **diploid** state. We say *most* cells because when it comes time to reproduce, the unfertilized seed and the pollen, called **gametes**, are formed by the splitting apart of the paired chromosomes during meiosis, forming a nucleus with a single set of chromosomes; the unpaired or **haploid** state. And just to make things complicated, true seeds have extra diploid tissue from the seed parent which merges with a haploid pollen nucleus to form the endosperm of a seed.

The fertilized endosperm therefore has 3 sets of chromosomes (two from the seed mother and one from the pollen father) and is **triploid**. This extra genetic material nourishes the germinating seedling. In rare instances a parent will not go through the normal splitting process of meiosis and as result the gametes are **unreduced**, donating the diploid number of chromosomes instead of the haploid.

Most rhododendrons get one set of chromosomes, denoted as **1x**, from each parent (female and male) resulting in two sets of chromosomes. They are commonly referred to as diploids, and denoted as **2x** (1x + 1x = 2x). However, some rhododendrons have four sets of chromosomes. These are commonly referred to as **tetraploids**, and denoted as **4x** (2x + 2x = 4x). **Triploids** have three sets of chromosomes and are denoted **3x**. **Pentaploids** have five sets of chromosomes and are denoted **5x**. Rhododendrons having more than two sets of chromosomes are referred to as **polyploids**.[1]

Although most rhododendron species are diploids, tetraploid rhododendron species do exist.[2] Individual triploid rhododendrons, appearing to be hybrids, sometimes occur naturally where diploid and tetraploid species of *Rhododendron* are co-located.[3] The term **neotetraploid** or **neopolyploid** refer to a recent hybrid whether man-made or natural that is a higher ploidy than the diploid state.

TRIPLOID R. 'GOMER WATERER' is the offspring of a triploid (R. 'Pink Pearl') and a parent of a triploid (R. 'Phyllis Korn')

SALLY & JOHN PERKINS

DISCOVERING: THE JOURNEY

In the fall of 1989, our rhododendron polyploidy journey unknowingly started when we overheard at a local Rhododendron Meeting, a statement Frank Mossman wrote in 1972 concerning his hybridization efforts with *Rhododendron occidentale*:

'We have found that Rhododendron occidentale *will cross with many other rhododendrons or azaleas if* Rhododendron occidentale *is the seed parent, but* Rhododendron occidentale *as a pollen parent produces few seed.'* [4]

We wondered why.

In the fall of 2011 we noted from reading the ARS online ejournal, that in 1972 Harold Greer wrote the following concerning his hybridization with *R.* 'Countess of Derby' to produce *R.* 'Trude Webster':

'If you are one of those who feels that there could be nothing outstanding produced in a pink rhododendron I would have been the first to agree with you. That was until I saw the first bud unfold on the original seedling of R. 'Countess of Derby' *selfed.'* [5]

Both Mossman and Greer had encountered the wonder accompanying the many puzzles presented by polyploid rhododendrons, so we were in good company.

Starting in the early 1990s, we unknowingly crossed deciduous azaleas involving different ploidy levels, leading, in 2010, to collecting samples of diploid, triploid and tetraploid rhododendrons for ploidy testing at the University of Coimbra in Portugal. Each step on this pathway revealed more about the wonderful world of ploidy in our own rhododendron garden.

Below is a summary of what we discovered, often based on the research, observations, and documentation of many others, about the ploidy of hybrid elepidote rhododendrons and the people encountered on our slow but wondrous journey. Before *you* take this journey imagine the following:

It is 1913 and a beautiful spring day in England, so what do you do? George V is the first Windsor King, Woodrow Wilson is serving his first term as President of the United States, and World War I is a future event. The two most popular rhododendrons in the world are *R.* 'Pink Pearl', an 1890s Waterer hybrid, and *R.* 'Cynthia', an 1850s Standish & Noble hybrid. On a beautiful spring day in 1913, if you are Henry 'Harry' White, a nursery manager in Sunningdale, England, you cross *R.* 'Pink Pearl' with *R.*

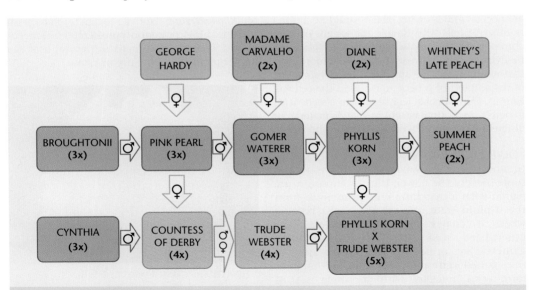

FIGURE 1: **GENERATIONAL BREEDING OF POLYPLOID HYBRID ELEPIDOTES** demonstrating that triploids can be fertile and can create a bi-directional pathway between ploidy levels

'Cynthia'. You later name a seedling from this cross *R.* 'Countess of Derby'.

In spring 1961, John Kennedy is the young handsome President of the United States and Vietnam is a country unknown to most Americans. On a beautiful spring day in 1961 if you are Harold Greer, living in Eugene, Oregon, you self *R.* 'Countess of Derby'. You later name a seedling from this cross *R.* 'Trude Webster'.

In spring 1969, Richard Nixon is the President of the United States and Watergate is simply an office building in the DC area. On a beautiful spring day in 1969 if you are Robert Korn in Renton, Washington, you place the pollen from *R.* 'Gomer Waterer', a 1900 Waterer *R.* 'Pink Pearl' hybrid, onto R. 'Diane'. You later name a seedling from this cross *R.* 'Phyllis Korn'.

In spring 1988, George H. Bush is the Vice President of the United States and Iraq is simply a country somewhere in the Middle East. On a beautiful spring day in 1988 if you are Jim Barlup, living in Bellevue, Washington, you cross *R.* 'Whitney's Late Peach' by *R.* 'Phyllis Korn'. You later name a seedling from this cross *R.* 'Summer Peach'.

In spring 2001, George W Bush is the President of the United States and the Twin Towers in New York City are still standing. On a beautiful spring day in 2001 if you are Jim Barlup, living in Bellevue, Washington, you cross *R.* 'Phyllis Korn' by *R.* 'Trude Webster' to create several viable offspring.

So what have you done by starting all this in 1913?

Well you took two fertile triploids from the 19th century, namely *R.* 'Pink Pearl' and *R.* 'Cynthia' and created a tetraploid, namely *R.* 'Countess of Derby'. You then selfed the tetraploid *R.* 'Countess of Derby' creating another tetraploid,

RHODODENDRON 'TAURUS' ('The Honourable Jean Marie de Montague' x *strigillosum*) is a triploid produced by unreduced gametes probably from the diploid seed parent   SALLY & JOHN PERKINS

namely *R.* 'Trude Webster'. You then placed pollen from the triploid *R.* 'Gomer Waterer' onto a diploid seed parent, namely *R.* 'Diane' and created a triploid, namely *R.* 'Phyllis Korn'. You then used the pollen of that triploid, *R.* 'Phyllis Korn' to create a diploid, namely *R.* 'Summer Peach'. You then placed the pollen of the tetraploid *R.* 'Trude Webster' onto the triploid seed parent *R.* 'Phyllis Korn' and produced a series of pentaploid seedlings *(see Fig. 1)*.

By doing so you ended the myth that triploids are always sterile and showed that triploids can, in fact, be both seed and pollen parents. Moreover, triploids, when used in hybridization, produce both reduced and unreduced gametes. You demonstrated that triploids provide a pathway for the bi-directional transfer of genes between diploids, triploids, tetraploids and pentaploids.

It took you a few beautiful spring days doing crosses, a few changes of names and addresses, nearly 90 years, and a team of young researchers at the University of Coimbra in Portugal to confirm your results but all in all not a bad piece of work!

THE PLOIDY OF NAMED HYBRID ELEPIDOTE RHODODENDRONS AS DETERMINED USING FLOW CYTOMETRY

SUMMARY

2x Diploids
1000 Butterflies
Alice
Anna (Lem, 1952) U
Betty Hume
Bibiani
Cheyenne *
Colonel Coen
Countess of Athlone
Diane
Duke Of York
Elegans
Everlasting *
Fantastica *
Furnivall's Daughter
Gillii
Gill's Triumph
Goldflimmer *
Goldsworth Orange #
Graf Zeppelin (van Nes, 1934) P
Horizon Lakeside
Hotei
Hurricane (Whitney, 1960) P
Isabel Pierce
Janet Blair *
J.G. Millais (Waterer, 1915) P
Jingle Bells #
Kathy Van Veen
Kupferberg #
Lady Bligh
Lady de Rothschild
Lady Eleanor Cathcart
Lem's Cameo
Loderi Venus
Madame Carvalho
Maxicat *
maximum Kalamity
Mindy's Love
Mother of Pearl (sport, 1925) P
Mrs A. T. de la Mare
Mrs Lindsay Smith
Mrs Furnival
Nancy Evans
Naselle

Norman Gill
Nova Zembla *
Olin O. Dobbs
Orange Leopard (Brack, 1988) P S
Peach Charm
Peach Recital (Barlup, 1996) P
Phipps Yellow
Pink Prelude
Polar Bear *
Puget Sound *
Red Olympia
Rendezvous (Hachmann, 1968) P S
Stony Brook (Brack, 1988) PS
Summer Peach (Barlup, 1988) P
Summer Wind (Barlup, 1996) P
The Honourable Jean Marie de Montague
   (van Nes, 1901) U
Viscy #
Voluptuous
Vulcan *
Vulcan's Flame *
White Pearl syn. Halopeanum
Wild Affair

3x Triploids
Anita Gehnrich (Waldman) UM
Anna Rose Whitney (Van Veen, 1954) F NM
August Lamken (Hobbie, 1942)
Beauty of Littleworth (Mangles, 1884)
Betty Wormald (Koster, 1907) F
Broughtonii (Broughton, 1840) F
Cotton Candy (Henny & Wennekamp, 1958)
   F UM
Cynthia (Standish &Noble, 1856) F
Dame Nellie Melba (Loder, 1926)
Django (Hachmann, 1985)
Ebony Pearl (sport, 1966)
El Camino (Whitney, 1976) NM
Gartendirektor Rieger (Hobbie, 1947)
Gomer Waterer (Waterer, 1900) F DM
Grace Seabrook (Seabrook, 1965) UM
Hallelujah (Greer, 1958)
Hank's Folly (Schannen) NM
Julia Caroline (Brockenbrough, 1990) NM

Lady of Spain (Lofthouse, 1966) NM
Lucky Strike (Van Veen, 1958) NM
Lydia (Greer, 1963) F NM
Markeeta's Flame (Markeeta, 1960) UM
Markeeta's Prize (Markeeta, 1970) UM
Opal Thornton (Thornton) NM
Pearce's American Beauty (Pearce, 1930) F
Phyllis Korn (Korn, 1969) F DM
Pink Pearl (Waterer, 1892) F DM
Platinum Pearl (Greer, 1983) F NM
Rothenburg (von Martin, 1944)
Rwain (Colombel, 1993) F NM
Solidarity (Schannen, 1969) F UM
Steredenn (Colombel) NM
Sugar Pink (Greer, 1960) NM
Super Dog (Bones) NM
Taurus (Mossman, 1962) F UM
Topsvoort Pearl (sport, 1935)
Val d'Aulnay (Croux and Fils, 1984) F
Van (Van Veen, 1930) NM

4x Tetraploids
Antoon van Welie (Endtz, 1930) 3X2
Brigg's Red Star (Briggs) T
Cherry Cheesecake (Briggs) T *
Countess of Derby (White, 1913) 3X3
diaprepes 'Gargantua' (Stevenson, 1923) †
Doreen Gale (Sanders) 4X4
Gentle Giant (Sanders, 1992) 4X3
Gorgeous George (Sanders) 4X4
Grand Slam (Greer, 1982) 4X3
Horizon Jubilee (Brockenbrough) *
Horizon Monarch (Brockenbrough, 1981) 2X4
Le Fouesnantais (Colombel, 1997) 4XQ
Legend (Barlup) 4X4
Lem's Monarch syn. Pink Walloper (Lem, 1965) 2X4
L Engin (de la Sablière) 4X2
Marinus Koster (Koster, 1937)
Point Defiance (Lem, 1970) 2X4
Summer Joy (Kehr) T
Super Nova (Briggs) T *
Trude Webster (Greer, 1960) 4x4
Very Berry (Greer, 1988) 4X2

KEY
F indicates a fertile triploid
T indicates a chemically induced tetraploid
P indicates a diploid with a polyploid ancestor
S indicates a diploid with a tetraploid parent
U indicates a diploid with a tendency to produce unreduced gametes
DM indicates a triploid resulting from a diploid parent
NM indicates a triploid resulting from a tetraploid parent
UM indicates a triploid resulting from 2 diploid parents
2X4 or 4X2 indicates a tetraploid resulting from a diploid and a tetraploid parent
3X2 indicates a tetraploid resulting from a triploid and a diploid parent
3X3 indicates a tetraploid resulting from 2 triploid parents
4X4 indicates a tetraploid resulting from 2 tetraploid parents
4X3 indicates a tetraploid resulting from a tetraploid and a triploid parent
4XQ indicates a tetraploid resulting from a tetraploid parent
* indicates flow cytometry ploidy testing was done by research team lead by Dr Ranney
# indicates flow cytometry ploidy testing was done by Tom Eeckhaut
(,) indicates the name of the hybridizer and date of cross.

† Noteworthy is the named form *R. decorum* ssp. *diaprepes* 'Gargantua'. There is no evidence that the subspecies *diaprepes* is tetraploid. ONLY the named form 'Gargantua' (selected from seed raised from Forrest 11958) has tested as tetraploid. To date, no elepidote species as a population has tested as tetraploid, but this could change.

R. **'BEAUTY OF LITTLEWORTH'** (*griffithianum* x *campanulatum*) is a triploid from 1884. The species R. griffithianum is involved in a number of older polyploid breeding programs

SALLY & JOHN PERKINS

Historical evidence indicates that by 1910 the triploids *R.* 'Betty Wormald', *R.* 'Beauty of Littleworth', *R.* 'Broughtonii', *R.* 'Cynthia', *R.* 'Gomer Waterer' and *R.* 'Pink Pearl' would have been on most people's lists of best elepidote rhododendrons.

In 1958, George Grace's list of best elepidote rhododendrons included all but one of these

TETRAPLOID *R.* 'LEM'S MONARCH' is a sister seedling of *R.* 'Point Defiance'

SALLY & JOHN PERKINS

triploids plus the tetraploids *R.* 'Countess of Derby' and *R.* 'Marinus Koster'.

In 2008, the Siuslaw Chapter of American Rhododendron Society included on their list of best elepidote rhododendrons the triploids *R.* 'Cynthia', *R.* 'Dame Nellie Melba', *R.* 'Grace Seabrook' and *R.* 'Taurus', and the tetraploids *R.* 'Grand Slam', *R.* 'Lem's Monarch', *R.* 'Horizon Monarch', *R.* 'Point Defiance' and *R.* 'Very Berry'.

By 2011, Rhododendrons of the Year, Proven Performers, Awards of Garden Merit and Best in Show trusses were added to the 'bests' mentioned above, taking in the triploids *R.* 'Anita Gehnrich', *R.* 'Anna Rose Whitney', *R.* 'Cotton Candy', *R.* 'Ebony Pearl', *R.* 'Gartendirektor Rieger', *R.* 'Hallelujah', *R.* 'Markeeta's Prize', *R.* 'Platinum

R. **'ANNA ROSE WHITNEY'** is a triploid produced from a diploid species (*R. griersonianum*) and tetraploid pollen parent (*R.* 'Countess of Derby')

SALLY & JOHN PERKINS

Pearl', *R.* 'Solidarity' and *R.* 'Super Dog', and the tetraploids *R.* 'Gentle Giant' and *R.* 'Trude Webster'.

R. 'Pink Pearl' won the first Award of Merit in 1897 and was selected Rhododendron of the Year in 2006 by the Southwestern Chapter of the American Rhododendron Society. In 1950, a large *R.* 'Cynthia', bred in 1858, was the first rhododendron planted in the Crystal Springs Rhododendron Garden. *R.* 'Trude Webster' won the American Rhododendron Society's first Superior Plant Award in 1971 and is still found on lists of Proven Performers for the west coast. *R.* 'Broughtonii', bred in 1840, is still considered to be among the best warm weather rhododendrons according to Don Burke who gardens in Australia.

In other words, over 25 of the 50 or so confirmed polyploid elepidote rhododendrons have appeared on lists of the best rhododendrons and once these polyploids appear on such lists they tend to make future such 'best' lists.

The following hybridizers have worked with or produced polyploid elepidote hybrids:

Barlup, Bones, Boulter, Bovees, Brack, Briggs, Brockenbrough, Broughton, Bruns, Colombel, Croux et Fils, de la Sablière, Drake, Elliott, Endtz, Evans, Farewell, Felix and Dijkhuis, Fennichia, Fujioka, Gill, Greer, Gehnrich, Hachmann, Hall, Hartman, Heinje, Henny and Wennekamp, Hobbie, Horlick, Horsley, Johnson, Kavka, Kehr, Korn, Koster, Larson, Laxdall, Lem, Loder, Lofthouse, Mangles, Markeeta, McCullough, Moynier, Mossman, Murcott, Naylor, Ostler, Patterson, Pearce, Perkins, Rabideau, Ragans, Reuthe, Sanders, Schannen, Seabrook, Shapiro, Smith, Standish & Noble, Stead, Stevenson, Stockman, Thacker, Thornton, van Nes, Van Veen, Vinson, von Martin, Waldman, Walton, Waterer, White, Whitney, Wilson, Weinberg & Smith, and Woodward.

TRIPLOID *R*. 'EBONY PEARL' is a sport of a triploid (*R*. 'Pink Pearl') that maintained the ploidy level   SALLY & JOHN PERKINS

DIPLOID *R*. 'THE HONOURABLE JEAN MARIE DE MONTAGUE' dates from 1901; it probably produces unreduced gametes

SALLY & JOHN PERKINS

Noteworthy is that more hybridizers have worked with confirmed elepidote polyploids than there are such confirmed polyploids. More importantly, some of the hybridizers on this list are best known for the polyploid elepidotes they have created. In fact, in a few instances polyploid elepidotes have been named in honor of a wife, a mother, or a grandparent.

Incidentally, Mossman, working with the diploid deciduous azalea species *Rhododendron occidentale*, discovered what Barlup later discovered working with hybrid elepidotes: diploids are much more likely to accept pollen from tetraploids than tetraploids are to accept pollen from diploids. We have addressed this topic in more detail elsewhere.[6]

Jim Barlup wrote the following about using polyploid elepidotes as parents:

'I continue to test the pollen and plants which I doubt for 3 or 4 years to determine their fertility or sterility. If you cross a diploid with tetraploid pollen you can achieve beautiful seedpods but their germination is very difficult. 3% seed germination for 'Point Defiance'. Obtained are both diploid or tetraploid offspring.'[7]

Breeding with polyploid elepidotes is not an easy task which explains why so few polyploids have been created to date, despite so many hybridizers having attempted to use them as parents.

Ron Naylor wrote the following about his best plant, *R*. 'Francis Augustus Storey', from a cross involving R. 'Point Defiance':

NAMED ELEPIDOTES SUSPECTED OF BEING POLYPLOID (AS YET UNTESTED)

Adriaan Koster
Aggie
Aibette
Alibaby
Annie E. Endtz
Arden Primrose
Ariel Sherman
Aristide Briand
Arnold Piper *
Arthur Ostler
Babar
Bellevue
Bernard Crisp
Bernard Shaw
Boskoop Concorde
Bruns Sirius
Canadian Beauty *
Cara Meg
Caruso
Castanets
Charis
Courtenay Duke
Dagmar
Denali
Diane Marie
Diane Titcomb
Direktor Siebert
Doctor A. Blok
Doctor Arnold W. Endtz
Doctor H.C. Dresselhuys
Don Juan
Donald Waterer
Doris Nolan
Double Drake
Dr. V.H. Rutgers
Edward Cornelius
Elizabeth Titcomb
Ester Grace
Eureka Maid
Fiona Wilson
Forever Violet
Fragrant Sensation *
Francis Augustus Storey *
Frentano
Friesland
Garnet

George Hardy
Germania *
Gill's Gloriosa
Goliath
Grab Ya *
Gunborg
Gwen Bell
Hachmann's Anastasia
Hachmann's Kristina
Haithabu
Halfdan Lem
Heat Wave
Heinje's Venezia
Helen Druecker
Hollandia
Horizon Serenity *
Ilam Apricot
Inheritance
Irmelies
Isadora
Isobel Baillie
Jan Dekens
Janet Ward
Jean Lennon
Jean Marie Variegated
Jeanne Yvonne
Jenice Coffey
Johnny Bender
Julie Titcomb
Justa Pink
Kareness
Kathe Heinje
Kathy Ann Pieries
Kay Too
KSW
Lady Longman
Leonardslee Giles
Lilian
Loder's White
Lou-John Gem
Madah Jean
Margaret Mack
Marion
Mary-Ed
Maureen Ostler
Melville

Miss Kitty
Mistake
Mrs E. C. Stirling (sister of
   Pink Pearl)
Newcomb's Sweetheart
Nicandra Newman
Orrie Dillie
Patricia Jacobs *
Peggy Bannier
Pink Goliath
President Kennedy
Pride of Roseburg *
Princess Debiann
Professor Hugo de Vries
Professor J. H. Zaayer
Qualicum's Pride
Queen Mary
Record
Reverend Paul *
Red Walloper *
Rhododendron niveum
Robert Korn
Romilda
Rotha
Scandinavia
Seraphine
Shalom
Shari Laurel
Sheer Enjoyment *
Sierra Sunrise
Sigrid
Souvenier de Doctor S. Endtz
Standishii
Titness Belle
TT116
Twins Candy
Virgo *
Vonnie Stockman
Walküre
Walloper *
Whidbey Island
White Swan
William Avery *

* Almost certainly polyploid

"Francis Augustus Storey' – Best of grex of four plants from weak germination. One died in 2000 and another in 2001.[8]

Dick Murcott wrote the following about the plant he calls 'TT116':

'TT116 – [('Jean Marie' x yakushimanum) x 'Grand Slam']. Only one seed from this cross germinated. Looks like a tetraploid. Pink. Looks like 'Trude Webster' but is definitely a seedling.[9]

Barlup, Murcott and Naylor each encountered both the wonder and puzzles presented by polyploid rhododendrons.

We have discovered for deciduous azaleas that seed produced from tetraploid x tetraploid normally has high rates of germination but germination from diploid x tetraploid crosses varies greatly but is normally low.

To read about Frank Abbott's encounter with the wonders of working with deciduous azaleas of different ploidy levels see 'Frank Abbott's Village of Azaleas'[10] or "Margaret Abbott' is a Tetraploid'.[11]

SUSPECTED PLOIDY

Despite having created the suspected polyploid list *(opposite)*, we believe that over 25% would not test as polyploid. However, *R*. 'Fragrant Sensation', *R*. 'Grab Ya', *R*. 'Pride of Roseburg' and *R*. 'Sheer Enjoyment', having both parents as tested tetraploids, are almost certainly polyploids. We

R. 'POINT DEFIANCE' is a tetraploid produced by the diploid seed parent's (*R*. 'Anna') unreduced gametes and the tetraploid pollen parent (*R*.'Marinus Koster')   SALLY & JOHN PERKINS

have marked using an * the dozen or so we think are the most likely (almost certainly) polyploids.

Most in this list are known to have at least one polyploid parent, be a sibling of a polyploid, or be a parent of one or more polyploids. However, both triploid and tetraploid hybrid elepidotes are known to be capable of producing diploid offspring when the other parent is a diploid. Many hybrids on our suspected polyploid list have one parent suspected of being a diploid. In other words, a diploid can have a polyploid parent or sibling. Moreover, two diploid parents can produce a polyploid offspring so having a polyploid offspring does not insure either parent is a polyploid.

If one excludes the known or suspected polyploid hybrids listed, creating a list of 100 suspected polyploid named elepidote hybrids, where more than 20% would test as polyploid, would be difficult. In fact, it is highly likely that most attempts at such a list of 100 named elepidote hybrids would include very few if any additional polyploids.

In other words, we speculate that nearly all (over 90%) named polyploid elepidote hybrids named prior to this article appear in this single article. This is almost certainly the case for polyploid elepidote hybrids named prior to 2000. The chances there were more than 200 polyploid elepidote hybrids named prior to that

R. 'MARGARET ABBOTT' is a tetraploid deciduous azalea produced from a diploid species (*R. prinophyllum*) and a tetraploid species (*R. calendulaceum*)   SALLY & JOHN PERKINS

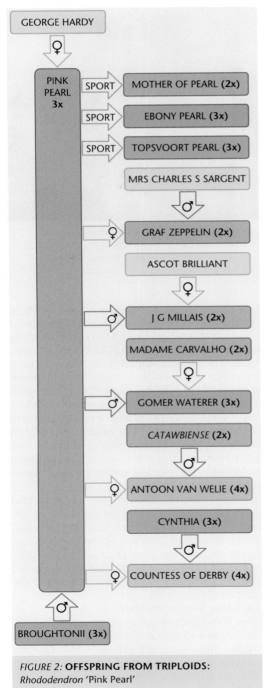

FIGURE 2: **OFFSPRING FROM TRIPLOIDS:**
Rhododendron 'Pink Pearl'

are low. The chances there were more than 50 tetraploid elepidote hybrids named prior to 2000 are even lower.

In short, there are no rules of thumb for guessing the ploidy of the offspring for hybrid elepidotes if the parents are of mixed ploidy levels or either parent is a triploid or pentaploid.

Diploid x diploid will almost always (but not always) create diploid offspring. Tetraploid x tetraploid will almost always (but not always) create tetraploid offspring. However, diploid x tetraploid and tetraploid x diploid, which are normally associated with producing triploid offspring, are known to often produce a combination of diploids, triploids, and tetraploids when working with hybrid elepidotes.

TRIPLOIDS, FERTILE TRIPLOIDS AND TRIPLOIDS AS THE PROGENY OF TRIPLOIDS

Triploids are normally believed to be produced by one of two mechanisms. Two diploids can cross where one diploid parent, instead of providing one set of chromosomes, provides two, resulting in an offspring that has 3 sets of chromosomes. This is commonly referred to as the **unreduced mechanism for creating triploids**.

Ploidy results suggest that triploids such as *R.* 'Anita Gehnrich', *R.* 'Grace Seabrook', *R.* 'Markeeta's Flame', *R.* 'Markeeta's Prize', *R.* 'Solaridity' and *R.* 'Taurus' were most likely created by this unreduced mechanism.

On the other hand, a diploid parent and a tetraploid parent can cross where the diploid parent provides one set of chromosomes and the tetraploid parent provides two sets of chromosomes resulting in an offspring with 3 sets of chromosomes. This is referred to as the **normal meiosis interploidy mechanism for creating triploids**.

Ploidy results suggest that triploids such as *R.* 'Anna Rose Whitney', *R.* 'Cotton Candy', *R.* 'El Camino', *R.* 'Hank's Folly', *R.* 'Julia Caroline', *R.* 'Lady of Spain', *R.* 'Lucky Strike', *R.* 'Lydia', *R.* 'Opal Thornton', 'Platinum Pearl', *R.* 'Rwain', *R.* 'Steredenn', *R.* 'Sugar Pink', *R.* 'Super Dog', and *R.* 'Van' were most likely created by this normal meiosis interploidy mechanism.

Triploids are commonly believed to always be sterile as both seed parents and pollen parents. Yet offspring are documented for triploids such as *R.* 'Anna Rose Whitney', *R.* 'Betty Wormald',

R. 'Broughtonii', 'Cotton Candy', R. 'Cynthia', R. 'Gomer Waterer', R. 'Lydia', R. 'Pearce's American Beauty', R. 'Phyllis Korn', R. 'Pink Pearl', R. 'Platinum Pearl', R. 'Rwain', R. 'Solidarity', R. 'Taurus' and R. 'Val d'Aulnay' (see Fig. 1).

Triploids such as R. 'Pink Pearl', R. 'Phyllis Korn', R. 'Rwain' and R. 'Taurus' appear to be partially fertile as both seed and pollen parents (see Fig. 2). In fact, triploids can be the progeny of triploids. Based on parental documentation, R. 'Broughtonii', R. 'Pink Pearl, R. 'Gomer Waterer' and R. 'Phyllis Korn' represent four consecutive generations of triploids (see Fig. 1).

Three sports of the triploid R. 'Pink Pearl' were ploidy tested: R. 'Ebony Pearl' and R. 'Topsvoort Pearl' tested as triploid whereas, intriguingly, R. 'Mother of Pearl' tested as diploid (see Fig. 2).

Diploids can be the progeny of triploids. The diploids R. 'Graf Zeppelin', R. 'Hurricane', R. 'J.G. Millais', and R. 'Summer Peach' are documented to have a triploid parent. In the case of R. 'Graf Zeppelin', the triploid R. 'Pink Pearl' is documented as the seed parent (see

R. 'HORIZON MONARCH' is a tetraploid produced from a diploid seed parent (R. 'Nancy Evans') and a tetraploid pollen parent (R. 'Point Defiance')   SALLY & JOHN PERKINS

Fig. 2). Although a diploid, R. 'Graf Zeppelin' exhibits characteristics often associated with named polyploids.

Tetraploids can be the progeny of triploids: R. 'Countess of Derby', a tetraploid, is documented to have 2 triploid parents, namely R. 'Pink Pearl' and R. 'Cynthia'. The tetraploids R. 'Antoon van Welie', R. 'Gentle Giant' and R. 'Grand Slam' are documented to have a triploid parent. In the case of R. 'Antoon van Welie', the triploid R. 'Pink Pearl' is documented as the seed parent (see Fig. 2).

Marc Colombel donated some of his suspected polyploid hybrid seedlings for testing. Noteworthy is that four seedlings of 'Rwain' x 'L'Engin' tested as tetraploid. R. 'Rwain' the seed parent, is a triploid. R. 'L'Engin', the pollen parent, is a tetraploid. Moreover, three seedlings of 'Horizon Monarch' x 'Rwain' tested as tetraploids but one seedling tested as triploid. R. 'Horizon Monarch' is a tetraploid.

Fig. 2 suggests that a triploid parent, for instance R. 'Pink Pearl', can produce offspring that are diploids, triploids and tetraploids. Fig. 1 suggests that pentaploids are also possible from a triploid parent.

In the 1930s, CJ Darlington showed that triploids could be fertile. Moreover Darlington confirmed a third mechanism for creating triploids. Darlington showed that, during

R. 'PEARCE'S AMERICAN BEAUTY' is an example of a very cold hardy triploid; the source of the higher ploidy is unknown

SALLY & JOHN PERKINS

meiosis, triploids chromosomes may split forming a bell-shaped curve distribution. This means that although there are a few cells formed with 1x and 2x chromosomes, most are closer to the midpoint of 1.5x. So in a few cases, a triploid parent can act as a diploid contributing 1 set of chromosomes or as a tetraploid contributing 2 sets of chromosomes.

Our ploidy results, when combined with the documentation of parentage, strongly suggest this third **distributive meiosis mechanism** does occur for fertile triploid elepidote rhododendrons.

Hans Eiberg has determined in controlled lab experiments that, for rhododendrons, hybrid triploid pollen is sometimes as viable as any hybrid diploid pollen.

TETRAPLOIDS AND DIPLOIDS AS THE PROGENY OF TETRAPLOIDS

Tetraploids such as R. 'Doreen Gale', R. 'Gorgeous George', and R. 'Legend' have been created by the normal meiosis mechanism where both parents are tetraploids.

Tetraploids such as R. 'Horizon Monarch', R. 'Lem's Monarch', R. 'L'Engin', R. 'Point Defiance' and R. 'Very Berry' may have been created by the unreduced mechanism of a diploid parent with the other parent being a tetraploid.

R. 'ANITA GEHNRICH' is a triploid probably produced by the diploid seed parent's (R. 'The Honourable Jean Marie de Montague') unreduced gametes   SALLY & JOHN PERKINS

Justin Ramsey's work with newly created neotetraploids suggests that such neotetraploids may experience irregular meiosis. Ramsey suggests that in some instances a neotetraploid may contribute only one set of chromosomes to the offspring. For the purposes of this article, we refer to this as the **super-reduced mechanism**.

Diploids such as R. 'Orange Leopard', R. 'Rendezvous' and R. 'Stony Brook' may have been created by this super-reduced mechanism. In the case of R. 'Rendezvous', the tetraploid R. 'Marinus Koster' is documented as the seed parent.

Noteworthy is that one seedling of R. 'Horizon Monarch' which had been open pollinated, tested as diploid. The actual plant of R. 'Horizon Monarch' that was the parent of this particular diploid seedling tested as tetraploid. Other seedlings from the same seedpod tested as tetraploid.

Our ploidy results suggest that tetraploids may produce diploid, triploid, tetraploid and pentaploid offspring.

NORMAL, UNREDUCED, SUPER-REDUCED AND DISTRIBUTIVE MEIOSIS: BY THE NUMBERS

A diploid rhododendron has 26 chromosomes. Normally a diploid rhododendron as a parent splits in half, contributing 13 chromosomes to the offspring.

A tetraploid rhododendron has 52 chromosomes. Normally a tetraploid rhododendron as a parent splits in half, contributing 26 chromosomes to the offspring.

A triploid rhododendron has 39 chromosomes. Half of 39 is between 19 and 20. Darlington showed that if a triploid having 39 chromosomes were to split, it would split mainly 19/20 but also, to ever decreasing occurrences, 18/21, 17/22, 16/23, 15/24, 14/25 and 13/26, where the splitting as 13/26 occurs the least. This splitting would form a bell shaped curve between 13 and 26.

Thus, in principle, for rhododendrons:

- diploid x diploid usually results in a diploid since 13 + 13 = 26
- tetraploid x tetraploid usually results in a tetraploid since 26 + 26 = 52
- diploid x tetraploid usually results in a triploid since 13 + 26 = 39

- diploid x unreduced diploid can in a few instances result in a triploid since 13 + 26 = 39.
- unreduced diploid x tetraploid can in a few instances result in a tetraploid since 26 + 26 = 52
- diploid x super-reduced tetraploid can in a few instances result in a diploid since 13 + 13 = 26
- diploid x triploid can in a few instances result in a diploid since 13 + 13 = 26 or in a triploid since 13 + 26 = 39
- triploid x tetraploid can in a few instances result in a triploid since 13 + 26 = 39 or in a tetraploid since 26 + 26 = 52

Noteworthy is that other researchers found that the offspring of triploids are often **aneuploids** (having an abnormal number of chromosomes). For rhododendrons, an aneuploid would have a number of chromosomes slightly more or less than 26 (2x), 39 (3x), 52 (4x), 65 (5x) or other multiples of 13 (x=13).

The unstable meiosis associated with triploids and neotetraploids most likely means that some of the rhododendrons listed above as diploids, triploids, or tetraploids do not have exactly 26, 39, or 52 chromosomes but instead may have a chromosome count close to these numbers. Flow cytometry being a method of weighting *sets* of chromosomes rather than counting the *number* of chromosomes is not well suited to separating **euploids** (a normal number of chromosomes) from aneuploids when the samples tested involve interactions between a wide range of species within the same genus.

SUMMARY

Named hybrid elepidote polyploid rhododendrons have played an important role in the garden for more than 150 years.

The physical characteristics associated with polyploid rhododendrons have proven to be highly desired by gardeners since their introduction by Broughton, Standish & Noble and Waterer.

The ploidy of more than 100 named hybrid elepidote rhododendrons is listed above.

Although to date all species of elepidote rhododendrons have tested as diploid, more than 50 named hybrid elepidote rhododendrons have tested as polyploids.

Approximately two-thirds of the named hybrid elepidote rhododendrons which tested as polyploids tested as triploids with the remaining third testing as tetraploids.

Triploids can be fertile as both seed and pollen parents. Triploids are able to produce diploid, triploids, tetraploid and pentaploid offspring.

Tetraploids are able to produce diploid, triploid, tetraploid and pentaploid offspring.

The mechanisms of normal, distributive, unreduced and super-reduced meiosis are discussed.

This research used as a foundation, work done by the following:

Hybridization of Rhododendron Elepidote Polyploids by Jim Barlup www.rhododendron.fr/articles/article35c.pdf

Rules of Engagement: Have Pollen – Will Travel by John and Sally Perkins http://rosebayblog.blogspot.com/2009/12/rules-of-engagement.html

Ploidy Levels and Relative Genome Sizes of Diverse Species, Hybrids and Cultivars of Rhododendron by Jeff R. Jones, Thomas G. Ranney, Nathan P. Lynch and Stephen L. Krebs http://www.holdenarb.org/education/documents/Jonesetal2007.pdf

Ploidy Breeding and Interspecific Hybridization in Spathiphyllum and Woody Ornanamentals by Tom Eeckhaut http://lib.ugent.be/fulltxt/RUG01/000/788/476/RUG01-000788476_2010_0001_AC.pdf

Meiosis in Polyploids Part I. Triploid and Pentaploid Tulips by W. C. F. Newton and C. D. Darlington http://www.springerlink.com/content/d017424p78822ll3/

Neopolyploidy in Flowering Plants by Justin Ramsey and Douglas W. Schemske http://www.botany.wisc.edu/courses/botany_940/07Polyploidy/papers/RamseySchemske02.pdf

Posts for each sample ploidy tested are available on the Rosebay Blog.

Posts have been grouped using tags to promote easy viewing of related posts.

Please weigh in by exploring these posts to discover the wonderful world of ploidy in the Rhododendron Garden.

http://rosebayblog.blogspot.com/search/label/U of Coimbra

ACKNOWLEDGEMENTS

We wish to thank the following people and organizations who donated samples for this research: John Abbott, Vivian Abney of East Fork Nursery, Charles Andrews, Living Collection of Arnold Arboretum, Natural Collection of Audra State Park, Living Collection of Bartlett Arboretum, Jim Barlup, Bruce Clyburn, Jane Brooks, Joe Bruso, Werner Brack, Ned Brockenbrough, Natural Collection of Canobie Lake, NH, Dick Cavender, Living Collection of Connecticut College Arboretum, Marc Colombel, Mike Creel, Al Fitzburg, Robert Fox, Harold Greer of Greer Gardens, George Hibben, Living Collection of Highstead Arboretum, Don Hyatt, Lindy Jackson of Appalachian Native Plants, Richard Jaynes of Broken Arrow Nursery, Doug Jolley, Fred Knippel, Living Collection of Longwood Gardens, Ron Miller, Dick Murcott, Michael Medeiros of Planeview Nursery, Portsmouth, RI John and Sally Perkins, Ron Rabideau of RareFind Nursery, Ellie Sather of Whitney Gardens, Natural Collection of Stoddard Blog, NH, John Thornton, Hendrik Van Oostand of Azaleatuin, Kathy Van Veen of Van Veen Nursery.

Sally & John Perkins

garden in Salem, NH, USA on a small wooded lot full of wildflowers and rhododendrons made possible by the excellent drainage, afforded by the slope down to the shoreline of Canobie Lake. Both have been members of the American Rhododendron Society Massachusetts Chapter for over 20 years and Sally is also the District 6 director. John is a software architect and Sally a part-time program manager for the US Department of Veterans Affairs research

José Cerca De Oliveira

is a Graduate Student in the Life Sciences Department at University of Coimbra, Portugal concentrating on the taxonomy and morphology of Portuguese flora

Mariana Castro

is a Masters Student in the Life Sciences Department at University of Coimbra, Portugal

Dr Sílvia Castro

is a Post-Doctoral Researcher in the Department of Life Sciences, Faculty of Sciences and Technology, University of Coimbra concentrating on plant-animal interactions (pollination and seed dispersal) and evolutionary dynamics of diploid-polyploid plant groups

Dr João Loureiro

is an Assistant Professor in the Department of Life Sciences, Faculty of Sciences and Technology, University of Coimbra concentrating on plant evolution

REFERENCES ■ 1. Understanding Polyploidy: Insights Into the Evolution and Breeding of Azaleas, Thomas G. Ranney & Jeff R. Jones – Mills River, North Carolina
http://www.ces.ncsu.edu/fletcher/staff/tranney/understanding_polyploidy2008.pdf
2. Rhododendron colemanii: A New Species of Deciduous Azalea (Rhododendron section Pentanthera; Ericaceae) from the Coastal Plain of Alabama and Georgia
http://www.ces.ncsu.edu/fletcher/mcilab/publications/zhou-etal-2008.pdf
3. Audra State Park: A Ploidy Haven
http://rosebayblog.blogspot.com/2010/09/audra-state-park-ploidy-haven.html
4. With Camera, White Umbrella, and Tin Pants. In *R. occidentale* Heartland. Frank Mossman, Vancouver, Wash. http://scholar.lib.vt.edu/ejournals/JARS/v26n4/v26n4-mossman.htm
5. R. 'Trude Webster' Harold Greer, Eugene, Oregon,
http://scholar.lib.vt.edu/ejournals/JARS/v26n2/v26n2-greer.htm
6. Rules of Engagement: Have Pollen - Will Travel. John and Sally Perkins, Salem, NH,
http://rosebayblog.blogspot.com/2009/12/rules-of-engagement.html
7. L'hybridation de rhododendrons élépidote polyploides. Jim Barlup,
http://www.rhododendron.fr/articles/article35c.pdf
8. Ron Naylor Rhododendrons http://219.88.101.105/e16.html
9. Selected Rhodo Seedlings. Rich Murcott. http://www.murcottgarden.com/select-seedlings
10. Frank Abbott's Village of Azaleas. John and Sally Perkins, Salem, NH,
http://rosebayblog.blogspot.com/2009/09/abbott-azaleas.html
11. 'Margaret Abbott' is a Tetraploid. John and Sally Perkins, Salem, NH,
http://rosebayblog.blogspot.com/2011/06/margaret-abbott-is-tetraploid.html
12. 'Pink Pearl' is a Fertile Triploid,
http://rosebayblog.blogspot.com/2010/10/pink-pearl-is-fertile-triploid.html

'Call of the wild' – Arunachal Pradesh through fresh eyes

TOM CLARKE

LATE MORNING IN THE PRISTINE FOREST BELOW THE HOOT LA, 2505m   TOM CLARKE

I CONSIDER MYSELF FORTUNATE to have been a professional gardener all my adult life, joining the National Trust as an apprentice some 20 years ago. I arrived at Trelissick Gardens in Cornwall eight years later and this was where I encountered my first rhododendrons. Little did I know at that time the impact this group of plants would have on me, both professionally and personally, in the following years. When it was suggested in 2009 that I should consider joining Keith Rushforth on a visit to the remote and mysterious Indian state of Arunachal Pradesh, my first thoughts were that not only was I about to realise a boyhood dream but that finally I would be able

to witness some of my favourite plants growing in their native habitat. I was even more excited to learn that amongst our party would be two fellow Rhododendron, Camellia and Magnolia Group members, both experienced rhododendron growers – Dick Fulcher and John Anderson, and the opportunity to spend time in the field for the first time in such distinguished company would be an offer I could not easily turn down.

The trip itself was to be a trek into the densely forested and mountainous border region between India and Burma, to the east of the sparsely populated Lohit river valley. This is in a range of mountains previously known as the

PRUNUS CERASOIDES **IN FLOWER,**
beyond the Udiat pass, 1500m   TOM CLARKE

Malay arch, a hitherto little explored wilderness of mountain peaks, cool temperate forest and sub-tropical valleys in the extreme east of India. Our objective was to pass through the low altitude hill jungle as quickly as we could, avoiding blister flies, leeches, spiders and poisonous snakes wherever possible, and on into the cooler temperate forest between 1500m and 3500m where we hoped to observe a whole range of temperate plants. In particular, I was looking forward to seeing my first rhododendrons growing in the wild.

After several false starts, including an unexpected night at Heathrow and a less than luxurious one in the heat of downtown Delhi, our journey began in earnest. By contrast, our second night in India was spent in a beautiful colonial bungalow in the immaculately manicured tea plantation of Manacotta in the Assam plains. Our arrival there coincided with the Hindu festival of Durga which seemed to involve the erection of makeshift shrines at the end of every street and the letting off of very loud fireworks (particularly before breakfast!)

The drive through Assam to the border with Arunachal Pradesh was predictably chaotic; our little Indian jeeps weaving constantly between pedestrians, goats, bicycles, bullock carts, mopeds, beautifully decorated lorries and, of course, cows. The countryside was a patchwork of tea plantations, rice paddies and water palm groves punctuated by small brightly coloured hamlets and villages, all with small gardens the like of which you see throughout the tropics.

It was lunchtime when we arrived at the state border whereupon our guide, Anong, promptly disappeared into the guardhouse, emerging, after a nervous wait on our part, with our permits. (Access to Arunachal Pradesh is still tightly controlled by the Indian authorities and an inner line permit is required in order to enter the state, due to its proximity to the disputed Chinese border to the North.)

Once inside Arunachal Pradesh the scenery changed dramatically and we were almost immediately plunged into the dense lowland monsoon forest that covers much of the approach to the hills. As the mist cleared, we were treated to our first glimpse of the distant hills as they began to rise up mysteriously from the sweltering plains. With afternoon drawing on, we slowly climbed in altitude, up some very windy and, at times, narrow roads until we crossed the Lohit river, a few miles above the point where it drains out into the Assam plains, and miles later becomes the mighty Brahmaputra, one of the great rivers of India.

We continued our climb up to the Udiat Pass which acts as a gateway into the Lohit valley and the distant hills beyond, and at 1600m commands a breath-taking view of the plains below. My excitement at finally arriving in the mountains was compounded by the sight of the first of several recognisable plants including *Betula alnoides*, *Hydrangea heteromalla*, *Debregeasia longifolia* and, in full flower, magnificent in the late afternoon light, was *Prunus cerasoides* looking slightly at odds surrounded by its sub-tropical neighbours.

Night falls suddenly in the hills and before long we were plunged into total darkness. At every violent swing of the jeep headlights through the dense forest I expected to see a big cat leaping out onto the jungle track or some other exotic animal's eyes shining in the vegetation. Eventually stopping at the bank of the Tidding river (a spot mentioned by Kingdon Ward in *A Plant Hunter in Tibet*), we made camp beside the ruined piles of one of the several bridges destroyed by the spring thaw. We were greeted by our hosts, who had been busy preparing for us the first of many superb camp fire meals, and when introduced, all appeared to be Anong's (our host and guide's) cousins.

Before I retired to my sleeping bag for my first night under canvas, I climbed down to the river bank and, as the Lohit river roared by on its journey from the Tibetan plateau to the Bay of Bengal, under a vast star-studded sky, the enormity of what I was doing and where I was slowly began to sink in.

We awoke to rain, had a hearty breakfast and quickly broke camp, eager to get on the road. We drove for the rest of the day through the spectacular tropical hill forest full of *Castanopsis*, tropical magnolias and bananas all dripping with vines, on a road reminiscent of the woodland walk back at Trelissick (in both quality and width), eventually arriving in the village of Hawai around mid-afternoon.

At 1500m it was still a long walk to the flora in which we were interested but as we had arrived before our tents, we took a stroll around the village, spotting *Castanopsis indica*, *Viburnum cylindricum* and an impressive *Quercus glauca*.

Anong arrived and promptly began to organise some of the local Mishmi men who would act as our porters and guides for the next ten days. After endless negotiations with the local hunters it was clear that Anong felt we would not have enough porters for the trek and he promptly headed back down the valley to find reinforcements, promising to catch us up the following day.

Our newly appointed local Mishmi guide, a hunter, introduced himself as Sochet and, in a flurry of activity, motioned us to follow him since this was where our trek was to

begin. To our disappointment, instead of climbing up, we headed down into the next valley, losing nearly 600m in altitude! We passed through stands of *Pinus kesiya* and over a rickety suspension bridge before arriving at the first of the two Mishmi villages we were to visit en route to the mountains. The village, called Kumblat, consisted of several traditional longhouses constructed of bamboo and reed, each surrounded by an immaculate sub-tropical garden growing beans, air potatoes, squashes, banana, cardamom and chillies, and fenced in by a split bamboo fence. As we sat around and waited for our bags to catch up, the locals very kindly found us firewood and offered us vegetables from their gardens. We, in turn, entertained them by showing off our various digital cameras, although they seemed more interested in Dick's magnificent beard than the miracle of digital photography!

As night fell it was hard to escape the feeling that, apart from the occasional roof-top solar panel, the scene can have changed very little from Kingdon Ward's visits to the region almost a century before.

Our gear finally arrived after dark and we made camp in the middle of the village, once again drifting off to sleep to the sound of the river roaring down its granite staircase into the

KUMBLAT VILLAGE, 965m   TOM CLARKE

valley below. We awoke to rain and left Kumblat, still without Anong, continuing our journey upwards, climbing a muddy and at times dangerous track to the second Mishmi village of Lapkrong which, at 1495m, was a little cooler, but equally wet. The village itself was much the same as the last with its gardens and traditional houses but in the centre was an abandoned longhouse, close to, if not slightly beyond, the point of collapse. This was to become our home for the next day and a half as we waited for Anong to arrive.

The Mishmi people inhabit much of the hill country between India and Burma and continue with a largely traditional way of life, which includes ritual animal sacrifice. Once an animal has been sacrificed the Mishmi like to adorn the interior of their houses with the skulls and jaw bones. When hung en masse along the beams they become blackened with soot and form an impressive centrepiece to any Mishmi home. Our makeshift home was no different; many of the skulls were recognisable but some were not and it made for interesting discussion

RHODODENDRON IRRORATUM and the hills beyond, 2090m   TOM CLARKE

at meal times as we tried to work out to whom they had once belonged.

Anong arrived after breakfast as did various porters throughout the rest of the day. By the time our last porter had appeared Anong decided it would be wise to delay our start until the next morning and, in order to dispel the inertia the was beginning to creep through our camp, we decided to take the opportunity to explore the thickly forested hill behind the village. We spent several hours climbing through thick vegetation, which began as sub-tropical hill jungle, becoming what may be best described as warm temperate forest and where we suddenly found ourselves surrounded by *Lithocarpus pachyphyllus*, *Lindera megaphylla*, *Alnus nepalensis*, *Rhus*, *Daphniphyllum* and at least five different species of *Araliaceae* above a forest floor carpeted with *Strobilanthes* and *Hedychium* species.

At exactly noon, seven days after leaving the UK, the first rhododendron was spotted. As the light struck the bright orange peeling bark it shone out like a beacon in the woods; its trunk

RHODODENDRON MOULMAINENSE **AFF** at 1600m
                    TOM CLARKE

was at least 10m tall and it was growing with only two or three of its own kind. Keith identified it as *Rhododendron moulmainense* aff. Although growing at a low altitude (1600m) and probably not hardy, even in Cornwall, it is hard to put into words the excitement of seeing my first rhododendron in the wild – a moment I will not easily forget!

We arrived back in the village soaked through to the skin – it had now been raining for three days straight and showed no sign of stopping. Despite this, we passed a very enjoyable evening in our deserted village house, drying our clothes by a fire mainly fuelled by the house itself – our cook SB was happily tearing down parts of the interior walls to keep it going! I retired to bed early, hoping that today's rhododendron would be the first of many and, as it turned out, I was not to be disappointed.

Leaving the relative comfort of the village behind us, we headed into the rain soaked hills to the east. Almost immediately we began to climb a steep and treacherous ridge through the forest, punctuated frequently by heart-stopping drops into the valley below – a pattern

to be repeated over the coming few days since the trail through the forest was little more than a hunter's track, virtually indistinguishable from the rest of the forest. We made camp on a ledge under a large rock escarpment and thankfully the rain ceased – the ledge was far too narrow to allow the pitching of any tents.

We awoke to the smell of wood smoke and the noise of pots and pans rattling together as our cook prepared another fine breakfast of fried eggs, porridge and pancakes, this time under very precarious conditions. The break in the rain continued and we were soon climbing again, gaining altitude under clear skies and sunshine and able, for the first time, to fully appreciate the view of the steep-sided wooded valley we had now entered. The forest was still predominantly evergreen with a canopy of *Lithocarpus*, oak and *Schefflera* and we were treated to a noisy tree-top display of Assam macaques, obviously annoyed by our presence in their forest! The vegetation was changing fast and we were soon amongst large stands of *Rhododendron irroratum* which quickly formed the understory to the ever-changing mix of larger trees. Once above 2200m

RHODODENDRON SINOGRANDE AND TSUGA DUMOSA around our campsite at Tongul, 2500m

TOM CLARKE

we began to climb into a fabulous mixed forest of *Tsuga dumosa*, *Betula utilis* and *Acer campbellii*, and as I turned a corner I came face-to-face with a superb *Rhododendron maddenii* growing out of a mossy stump by a small stream – I really felt the adventure was just beginning!

We made camp that night on a ridge, among a majestic grove of *Tsuga dumosa* at around 2525m, a place our guide called Tongul. As we warmed ourselves around the fire the atmosphere was full of anticipation for the following day, since we were clearly about to enter the cooler temperate forest. We retired to our tents with the ominous sound of thunder rumbling around in the surrounding valleys.

COOL TEMPERATE FOREST approaching Sayang Jang campsite, 2800m   TOM CLARKE

The weather deteriorated throughout the next day, as did the trail, which was by now becoming lethal; one false move or broken root could send you several hundred metres down into the valley below with little hope of salvation. Sonshet did his best to make the way as safe as possible or at least do running repairs to some of the many rotting timbers we relied on to negotiate this truly terrifying path.

The forest was by now dripping with moss and lichen and although the overstory was still hemlock, the understory was feeling more and more familiar, with *Rhododendron maddenii* ssp. *crassum*, *Stachyurus himalaicus*, *Schefflera*,

RHODODENDRON REX SSP. FICTOLACTEUM at 2800m   TOM CLARKE

Vaccinium, *Gaultheria* and *Lindera*, and, crossing a small ridge at 2425m, I spotted *Rhododendron sidereum*, at first growing here and there amongst the shrubs just mentioned, but, as I rounded a bend in the path, they began to form a forest of large trees; in spring they must be a magnificent sight. At the same time we began to spot the occasional *R. sinogrande*, but soon they were forming large trees with single stems up to 7m tall whilst others formed dense thickets, layering themselves and growing epiphytically on stumps of their own kind.

We traversed the site of a recent landslide and camped for the night in what can only be described as a plant hunter's paradise, surrounded, as it was, on all sides by majestic *R. sinogrande*, *Ilex nothofagifolia*, whitebeams, *Acer*, *Quercus semicarpifolia* and *Hydrangea heteromalla*. On entering our tent for the first time that evening we even found *Rhododendron fulvum* happily growing inside the porch!

The next day was spent in the rain, exploring the forest around our campsite where we encountered *Tetracentron sinensis*, *Acer wardii*, *Rhododendron crinigerum*, *R. arizelum* and our first silver firs, hinting at things to come. As the rain fell on our tent, Keith reflected on the altitude at which the rain would be falling as snow – a sharp reminder that our objective – climbing the Hoot La pass, above 4000m – was still several days' walk away.

By now we were approaching halfway round the circular route back to Hawai, although our local guide seemed unsure how long the return journey would take us (and the exact route!) Life in camp had settled into a steady routine: our day began around 5.00am with bed tea, which, as the name suggests, is a cup of extremely sweet, milky tea and, if you are lucky, a biscuit, served in your sleeping bag. There was then about an hour to sort out our gear and wash (by this stage strictly optional) before breakfast was served and our small, but adequate, packed lunch was presented to us individually (normally leftover breakfast and a hardboiled egg) – mine seldom made it past 10.00am, tea-time for gardeners the world over! We left camp around 7.00am and walked and botanised en route for the rest of the day. Once dismantled, our camp soon overtook us to be re-established several hours in advance of our arrival and always near fresh water. We followed the trail of broken twigs and footprints, wandering into camp (if we were lucky) before nightfall, by which time, for the most part, our evening meal was prepared.

Our porters were split into three distinct groups, firstly Anong and his cousins and cooks, mainly members of the Arbor tribe, who took fantastic care of all our needs from cooking, to erecting and dismantling our tents each evening, camping alongside us throughout our trip, even on occasion taking us fishing if required! The local Mishmi porters and guide, and several local hunters were responsible for getting us from A to B in one piece, repairing or creating bridges etc along the way. They normally camped in the forest several minutes' walk away and cooked their own food (apparently, curried monkey is not all it's cracked up to be). The third group was comprised of Indian, Nepali, and Mishmi men from the Tezu (back down on the plains) employed by Anong when it was clear that there were insufficient locals to support our trek. These guys were rather more urbane than the local Mishmis and were clearly a little nervous of their heavily armed countrymen –they made their camp closer to ours than the Mishmis.

The following morning started fine, but soon clouded over and the, by now, characteristic drizzle began to fall. We had set out early because our guide knew it would be a long day's walk to the next level camping site. We crossed a large waterfall and followed the Lapti river for several hours, through large forests of *R. rex* ssp. *fictolacteum* draped in festoons of moss. *Abies delavayi* had become the dominant tree species and the air was noticeably thinner and colder. We had climbed to around 3000m and there were rhododendrons everywhere and, on what appeared to be the site of a recent landslide, I recorded numerous species including *Rhododendron hookeri*, *R. glaucophyllum*, *R. tephropeplum*, *R. piercei*, *R. crinigerum*, *R. calostrotum* and *R. arizelum*. Alongside the rhododendrons, *Acer wardii*, *Larix griffithii*, *Juniperus coxii* and several deciduous trees, including species of *Sorbus*, birch, alder and *Magnolia globosa* made for a fabulous sight.

We made camp by the river and eventually succeeded in lighting a fire large enough to keep away the local wildlife and, after an hour of comparing notes with the rest of the team, a well-deserved early night was had by all.

COLD MOUNTAIN FOREST, at 3092m near Dong La campsite   TOM CLARKE

RHODODENDRON PRAESTANS in a forest of
Abies, 3305m   TOM CLARKE

Over breakfast, Sonchet revealed to Anong that he feared we were falling behind schedule, confessing that he was unsure how long it would take us to cross the pass and return to Hawai – several days of hard walking would be required if we were to get back in good time.

We struck camp early, eager to get on and soon found ourselves following the Lapti river as it flowed through a deep gorge with steep granite cliffs on either side, interspersed with waterfalls and wooded ravines. The forest was thinning out and as we climbed and the understory grew less and less dense, we passed *Rhododendron thomsonii* (at around 3330m) along with *R. lepidotum*, *Ribes* spp, and *Spirea*. Eventually we entered a valley, clothed with *Abies delavayi*, its understory comprised entirely of *Rhododendron praestans* – a truly memorable sight.

Camp was made on a small plateau amongst a stunted forest of silver fir, under the snow-capped mountains 1000m above us. As the light slowly faded, the temperature rapidly fell below freezing and we soon took to our tents. The following morning our campsite was covered with frost which lifted as the sunlight slowly filled the valley. As we headed up into an alpine meadow, with a high peak on either side, we wandered through drifts of *R. thomsonii*, *Rosa omeiensis*, swathes of *Meconopsis* and *Podophylla* spp, and by 8.00am we were well above the tree line. Continuing the climb through the, by now, stunning alpine landscape, it seemed rather like a Scottish mountainside except dwarf rhododendrons, such as *Rhododendron lepidotum* and *R. calostrotum,* replaced the heathers. A boggy stream flowed down the mountainside, surrounded by carpets of *Iris*, *Meconopsis* and large drifts of *Diapensia himalaica*, the valley ending abruptly with a wall of granite, flanked on either side by two much higher peaks, the lowest point of the ridge between the two forming the long-anticipated Hoot La pass.

The route suggested by our guide at first seemed impossible to climb but on closer inspection was fairly straightforward and afforded an unforgettable view back down the valley towards the previous night's camping ground. The fine weather appeared to be holding

PASSING THROUGH THE ALPINE MEADOW, 3900m
                                                    TOM CLARKE

THE AUTHOR (*RIGHT*) **AND FELLOW GROUP MEMBER, DICK FULCHER,** enjoy the view from the Hoot La summit, 4100m   TOM CLARKE

and as we neared the summit the panorama was truly breath-taking – the snow-covered peaks of what Kingdon Ward described as the 'Lohit Irrawaddy divide' lay before us in what must now be one of the last great unexplored areas of Asia. To stand and look out over hundreds of square miles of virgin mountain peaks, wooded ravines and river valleys, with the Burmese alps as a backdrop, was another moment I will never forget and Cornwall felt a long way off indeed.

Our euphoria at crossing the Hoot La was, however, short-lived for in the swift and disorientating descent into the thickly wooded valley below, our group became separated. I spent the best part of an hour and a half wandering alone through another vast forest of *Rhododendron praestans* until, quite by chance, I found our cook, SB, also lost but apparently unfazed by our predicament. We continued to descend at high speed until, again by chance, we happened upon a few more lost porters who by some miracle found a trail of fresh footprints in the compressed humus which eventually led us to our campsite within a large thicket of *R. arizelum*.

Porters continued to arrive throughout the afternoon and by nightfall they were amazingly all accounted for (how they all found the camp was a mystery, under the circumstances). We were, however, still missing several group members but, thankfully, they arrived, albeit long after dark, exhausted from the day's adventure; we had after all descended well over 1000m in just a few hours.

The mood in camp at breakfast was more subdued (after the highs of the last few days) and our guide told Anong that we needed to make up even more time and would have another long day of walking ahead of us, with little time for botanising. And so it was to be; we were now well back into the cool temperate forest and although we passed *R. sinogrande*, *R. maddenii* and a solitary *R. auriculatum*, the temperate woody plants were slowly replaced with aromatic laurels, *Lithocarpus*, *Araliaceae* and other evergreens. The going was hard, and after crossing countless waterfalls, landslides and river beds we finally camped under a large *Lithocarpus*, exhausted from our hike.

Yet another long walk the following day took us through the now familiar forest interspersed with a few large groups of *Rhododendron irroratum* aff. Around mid-day we reached an abandoned village, overgrown with a maze of giant bamboo; the first sign of any human activity since leaving

THE BRIDGE TO HALAI KRONG with 60ft *Dendrocalamus* species, 1139m   TOM CLARKE

THE INTREPID JOHN ANDERSON TESTS THE BRIDGE TO HALAI KRONG!   TOM CLARKE

Lapkrong ten days before and a very welcome sight indeed. Several more hours of hard walking took us down into a sub-tropical valley full of *Ficus*, banana and *Pandanus*, all hanging thick with climbers. The woodland path, edged with *Strobilanthes*, gingers, *Globoa* and orchids led down further to a crystal clear river where, after a much overdue wash, we crossed over on a suspension bridge and came to the Mishmi village of Halai Krong. We spent the night there, camped on the village green, much to the annoyance of the village drunk but to the general amusement of everyone else.

From Halai Krong it was matter of a short walk back to Hawai, where, after some confusion, our vehicles collected us and we began the slow and, at times, treacherous drive back to the heat and humidity of the Assam plains and the normality of our everyday lives – the adventure was over.

When I set out on this trip I had simply hoped that I would see some plants of interest; never in my wildest dreams did I imagine the wealth and variety of flora that we experienced in this one small corner of India. It is hard to express the importance of an experience like this for a working horticulturalist; the chance to witness first hand a group of plants, so important in any woodland garden, growing in the wild, has had a huge impact on my understanding of them and their requirements. Moreover, it has inspired me to research a whole range of genera I previously knew little about and has reinforced my belief in how lucky I am to have chosen a career in horticulture.

ACKNOWLEDGEMENTS

I would like to thank the Royal Horticultural Society for their generosity in supporting me with a Blaxall Valentine Award as well as the Rhododendron, Camellia and Magnolia Group for their additional financial support without which my trip would have been impossible and, in particular, Pam Hayward, Keith Rushforth and John Lanyon for their advice and support.

Tom Clarke

is Head Gardener at Trelissick Garden in Cornwall

Rhododendron arboreum –
Monarch of the Himalayas PART TWO

TONY SCHILLING VMH

MAGNIFICENT TREES OF *RHODODENDRON ARBOREUM* cloak entire hillsides with colour in April, seen here from the village of Ghorepani in Central Nepal   IZABELA SAJDAK, Edinburgh

SIR JOSEPH HOOKER (1817–1911)

SOME 19 YEARS AFTER Edward Gardner completed his posting in Kathmandu, Joseph Hooker, encouraged and assisted by Lord Dalhousie (Governor General of India), carried out two Himalayan expeditions, firstly in E Nepal in 1848 then in neighbouring Sikkim the following year.

His autumn journeys in E Nepal were prompted by his frustrations regarding entry to Sikkim which were caused by the obstructive Rajah of Sikkim. Even then his alternative plan for Nepal was only eventually made possible by way of Brian Hodgson's friendship with the ruler of Nepal, Jang Bahadur.

When permission to enter Sikkim eventually did come about, Hooker's travels and collecting activities were frequently obstructed and delayed by the Rajah, who on one occasion actually effected the temporary imprisonment of both Hooker and Archibald Campbell (British Political Agent to Sikkim). In his *Indian Journal* Hooker *(BELOW)* recorded that he and Campbell were *'seized, guarded and interrogated with intimidation and sent to separate tents.'*

His adventures and hardships were many but because of his total dedication to scientific research and his insatiable appetite for botanical discovery he persisted and prevailed against all the odds. Put quite simply, his accomplishments became and remain today a classical part of botanical history.

Whilst not belittling the achievements of Hardwicke, Hamilton, Wallich or Gardner, Hooker was without question the first of the really great rhododendron collectors. During his Himalayan travels in 1848/9 he collected, sketched and described no fewer than 36 species, 28 of which were new to science. Before his input of new 'rhododendron blood' only 33 species were available to Western gardeners and his discoveries, therefore, more than doubled the number in cultivation. Amongst this number was the noble *Rhododendron arboreum*, and his various introductions of this species enabled the horticultural world to realise for the first time the enormous gene-pool and potential of this plant. In fact, Hamilton's deep-red low altitude and tender introduction had given but a single 'snapshot' of what was actually out there in the vast Himalayan chain. Ironically, as time went by the botanical world would come to appreciate that Hooker's collections were in themselves further 'snapshots' of the whole picture made up from this variable and wide-ranging species.

It should be noted here that William Griffith made a four and a half month journey to the eastern Himalayan kingdom of Bhutan during 1838 and later, in 1843, sent collectors into Sikkim. However, there does not appear to be any evidence of either of these pre-Hooker expeditions 'flagging up' *R. arboreum* in any shape or form.

Although Hooker's collections of *R. arboreum* were significant in number and variable in colour form, any references regarding the species in his *Himalayan Journal* are not as noteworthy. Whilst collecting along the Singalila Ridge on the Nepal/Sikkim border in the company of a local resident (Charles Barnes) he wrote of coming upon specimens *'in appalling weather at 8000ft growing with* R. argenteum (grande) *and* R. barbatum.' Apart from this he wrote very little else of specific interest other than recording that *R. arboreum 'was common at about 5000–6000ft especially on dry slopes of mica-slate rocks.'* Brief notes contrasting dramatically with the impact his collections would make on Western gardens.

HOOKER'S LEGACY

Hooker's discoveries in Nepal and Sikkim would have been enough in themselves but he sent his enthusiasm and his plant material back home to Kew where the hard won results of his labours were successfully raised and spread to the far corners of the earth. Although the term 'networking' was not a recognised part of the English language at that time, Joseph Hooker and his father Sir William were without doubt excellent champions of the technique.

Records at Kew confirm that young plants of rhododendrons were distributed to nurserymen, individuals and botanic gardens throughout the temperate world (Forrest, 1996), Kew's records give details of the recipient as well as the name and number of species dispatched. Among the British names was JR Gowen, a gentleman of

RHODODENDRON ARBOREUM 'FERNHILL SILVER'   © PAINTING BY WENDY WALSH
From *Irish Florilegium: Wild and Garden Plants of Ireland* introduction by Ruth Isabel Ross, Thames & Hudson Ltd, London

independent means who supervised the rhododendron breeding for the Earl of Carnarvon at Highclere, near Newbury. Another was Sir Charles Lemon of Carclew in Cornwall, who on 5th December 1851 received young plants of well over a dozen different species including *Rhododendron arboreum*. From Carclew plants of various forms of *R. arboreum* were sent on to the garden at Heligan where John Tremayne had commenced planting in 1851. Seeds were also sent out to other Cornish gardeners. One of these was Mr Shilson of Tremough, near Penryn, who obtained seeds directly from Sir William Hooker at Kew. Richard Gill (Shilson's head gardener) stated in his article 'Himalayan Rhododendrons' that *R. arboreum* was *'present in all its varieties'* and by 1898 one had attained a height of 8.3m. Other specimens raised from Hooker's original introductions survive to this day in Westcountry gardens, but records are sadly lacking in many cases – if only plants could talk!

In Scotland, Hooker's introductions were particularly successful along the Gulf Stream-influenced west coast, most notably at Stonefield Castle and Kilmory Castle in Argyllshire, as well as further south at Lochinch, Castle Kennedy in Dumfries and Galloway. The latter plantings were made by the 10th Earl of Stair from material donated by Sir William Hooker and have since reached majestic proportions.

It is recorded that David Moore of Glasnevin Botanic Gardens in Ireland received material from Hooker's collections and some of this was passed on to the Darley family's garden at Fernhill, Co. Dublin. There they thrived and reached impressive stature, one particular tree being considered worthy of clonal distinction, namely *R.* 'Fernhill Silver'.

The gardens of southern England are renowned for their woodland plantings but many of them do not date back as far as the mid-1850s. In addition, planting records are all too often sketchy, or worse still, absent. However, Westonbirt in Gloucestershire does have specimens of *R. arboreum* which are said to have been raised from Hooker's seed. Another possible exception is the fine plant of a hardy blood-red form which grew at South Lodge near Horsham in West Sussex; its continuing existence remains to be confirmed. If so, it would be of particular interest as the colour form is seldom hardy in the Home Counties. Unfortunately, a similarly good colour form at Wakehurst Place was destroyed following the great storm of October 1987.

Hooker's rhododendrons were often sent overseas in glazed cases. One such despatch was sent to Dr Asa Gray in Massachusetts, USA as *'a close box by Mail Steamer from Liverpool'* (Forrest,1996). Others were sent in similar manner to various recipients in Australia and New Zealand. However, the most bizarre despatches must surely be two separate sendings to Jamaica in the West Indies. The first went to a Mr Smith on 30th September 1851 whilst the second was despatched to Sir Henry Barkly (Jamaica's Governor General) on 14th September 1853.

These sendings obviously succeeded as it is well recorded (D Leach et al) that a fine grove of *R. arboreum* exists in the Blue Mountains above Kingston. Frustratingly, the details of how and when this planting became established remains unanswered.

SUBSEQUENT INTRODUCTIONS

One only has to browse through the *RHS Rhododendron Handbook 1998* and elsewhere to realise that there were other relatively early collectors working in the Himalayas.

Viscount Falmouth has recorded (*Rhododendrons with Magnolias and Camellias*, 1976) that one of his mature Tregothnan specimens labelled as *Rhododendron arboreum* ssp. *delavayi* can probably be linked to seed brought back by Sir Francis Younghusband on his return from the British Political Mission to Lhasa in 1904/5. Assuming this connection to be correct it must surely stand as a significant historic record of introduction even if the subspecific detail may be open to question.

Perhaps the most interesting was Lieutenant FM Bailey (*Rhododendron baileyi* honours his name) who, after spending the winter months of 1912 in Mishmi territory, set off northwards in the company of Captain HT Morshead heading for Tibet. It is recorded (Allen, 1982) that when they emerged some six months later onto the Assam plains south of Bhutan *'they looked more like tramps than British officers.'*

During the course of their exploration they had virtually brought the prolonged mystery of the Tsangpo-Brahmaputra river gorge connection to an end. This spectacular defile (one of the deepest and longest on Earth) was until that time one of the great unsolved mysteries of the Himalayas. However, in view of its complex topography, they were unable to penetrate certain parts of the gorge and even today this *'last great Asian adventure'* is incomplete and will remain so until a continuous land journey from the Assam valley to the Tibetan plateau is undertaken.

During their return via the Nyamjang Chu on the Bhutan/

VENERABLE *RHODODENDRON ARBOREUM* F. *ALBUM* at Stonefield Castle, Argyll and Bute, probably an original Hooker seedling
KRISTIAN THEQVIST

BLOOD RED *RHODODENDRON ARBOREUM*,
Kohima, Nagaland in NE India　　　　DAVID SAYERS

Assam border they made two collections of *R. arboreum* which are documented as Bailey No 4 and Bailey No 5. Both these numbers are to be found in the collections of the Royal Botanic Gardens, Edinburgh and Windsor Great Park. Bailey No 4 was given the name *morsheadianum* by Millais in honour of Bailey's fellow travelling companion and in some publications the name has achieved clonal recognition viz. 'Morsheadianum'. Millais described the distinct selection as having leaves *'with a burnished, very close indumentum resembling that of* R. insigne *and with deeply impressed lateral veins.'* Some ten years later Kingdon Ward reintroduced material from the same area (KW6403) but this is listed in the *Rhododendron Handbook* as *R. arboreum* ssp. *delavayi*. Recent indications suggest that KW6403 is represented in the collections at Borde Hill, West Sussex and Exbury Gardens, Hampshire.

Bailey was a remarkable man who was known to push the boundaries of his agreed official duties. On more than one occasion when *'working on the fringes of officialdom'* he would return not knowing whether he would be congratulated or castigated! After retirement he returned home and died in Scotland in 1967. Morshead was also a colourful character being *'of modest stature, small, dark and as hard as nails, with extraordinary powers of physical endurance.'* In 1921 he participated in the first Mount Everest expedition but, sadly, he later came to a tragic end, being mysteriously murdered whilst out riding in Burma (Myanmar).

Other early collections of *R. arboreum* were carried out by GH Cave c1914, R Cooper 1914/15, G Forrest 1912/14 (as var. *delavayi*), Kingdon Ward 1921 (as var. *delavayi*), J Rock 1923/24 (as var. *delavayi*) and Ludlow and Sherriff 1936. The least well known of these is George Cave (*Cotoneaster cavei* honours his name) who was a personality whose work has, over the years, become rather lost in the shadows in spite of living to the great age of 95. His accomplishments are too many to fully record here, but after a period at Kew he moved to Calcutta Botanic Gardens before taking up the curator's post at the Lloyd Botanic Garden, Darjeeling where he remained for 24 years. He spoke several dialects of Tibetan and Bhutanese, climbed to 6096m collecting plants and even received a Tibetan teacup from the Dalai Lama as a token of gratitude. Specimens, papers and archives of his work are kept at the Royal Botanic Garden, Edinburgh (Watson, *pers comm*) and a representative of *R. arboreum* (Cave 6715) is held within the collections at the Younger Botanic Gardens, Benmore.

In the company of WW Smith he collected in the Zemu valley of Sikkim in July and their report of 1911 is said to form the most important reference to the flora of the area (Lang, 1991).

Following these various post-Hooker collections the flood gates regarding additional introductions of *R. arboreum* accelerated inordinately. In consequence, the boundaries of our understanding of the species in the broadest sense have extended accordingly. In some respects this continues even today and our appetite for collecting this variable species appears to have no final resolution.

TWO OF THE MANY COLOUR VARIANTS OF *RHODODENDRON ARBOREUM* **SSP.** *CINNAMOMEUM*
set against the Annupurna mountains of Central Nepal   GREG WILLIS

NATURAL DISTRIBUTION AND VARIATION

The genus *Rhododendron* is a primitive one of ancient origin and *R. arboreum* could well be amongst the oldest species of all since the massive proportions it achieves imply primeval beginnings. This statement is supported by the fact that it constitutes a number of complex and frequently ill-defined subspecies and varieties. It also has a truly vast distribution pattern spanning some 1500 miles (2415km) or more along the temperate corridor of trans-Himalayan Asia, and exhibits a remarkable altitude tolerance ranging from 1500m to over 3600m. Its longevity and potential for epicormic regrowth adds further to the argument.

Ranging from the Garhwal region of northwest India through Nepal, Sikkim and Bhutan, it spreads onwards as far as Upper Burma (Myanmar) as well as branching off northeastwards into southeast Tibet and southwest China. In Burma it stutters across a series of discontinuous uplands before it seemingly fades away in Thailand, close to the border of Vietnam. As well as this it occurs in two completely disconnected regions, namely the Nilgiri Hills of Tamil Nadu in southern India and the upland regions of Sri Lanka.

This inconsistent and gradual merging of botanical characteristics is known as a 'cline' (Huxley, 1938), a term which can be best expressed as a character gradient or a continuous trend from one taxonomic group to another. To delve deeply into detailed analysis regarding the *precise* taxonomic divisions of this species is to tread hazardous ground! In fact a more classical case for 'splitters' and 'lumpers' to declare war over is difficult to imagine, although *Betula utilis* is a very similar example. Much has been published regarding this dilemma and having personally observed the species in the mountains of Nepal, Bhutan and Yunnan I can but agree unreservedly with the conclusion Peter Cox published in *The Larger Rhododendron Species*. After weighing up the balance of opinion between Davidian and Chamberlain he states that *'although their respective diverse opinions may be useful horticulturally they are unsatisfactory taxonomically apart from those isolated geographically'* (viz. ssp. *nilagiricum* and ssp. *zeylanicum*). He goes on to state the he *'accepts the classification of Chamberlain as making the best compromise of a difficult problem.'* Whilst it is tempting and intellectually intriguing to 'split' it is without doubt an inevitable short cut to exasperation. Conversely, to 'lump' too simplistically is far too compromising. As long ago as 1850 Hooker and his contemporary Thomas Thomson deplored the *'prevailing tendency to exaggerate the number of species and to separate the accidental forms by trifling characters.'* At the time they were compiling the first volume of *The Flora of India* and still, some 160 years later, one continues to ponder the subject. When Hardwicke first came across the species in 1796 he little realised what he was starting. One is tempted to suggest that the enigma is akin to a long distance runner chasing a vanishing horizon!

Having referred already to the probability of exasperation over these issues it is impossible not to add a quote from Steve Hootman of the Rhododendron Species Foundation, Washington, USA who, having become confused by the diversity of *R. arboreum* and the accompanying natural hybrids in the hills of Nagaland, NE India, wrote *'what a promiscuous bunch they all are. Retaining critical intellect while scrambling up steep, muddy, slippery slopes through leech-festooned herbage … takes the romance out of plant hunting.'*

It may seem pointless to detail all the various subspecies and varieties within these notes as they are well documented elsewhere (Chamberlain, Cox et al) and pontificating should perhaps cease here.

However, such is the variety of distribution it may be of interest to mention in general terms the different ecological niches each entity occupies.

Rhododendron arboreum ssp. *arboreum* Usually occurs in open or mixed warm or cool temperate forest between 1850–3600m. Lower altitude forms seem to be fairly drought tolerant. Garhwal (NW India) → Sikkim → central Bhutan. Flowers typically blood-red.

R. arboreum ssp. *cinnamomeum* In open temperate to sub-alpine regions amongst *Abies* and *Betula* between 2400–3650m. Central Nepal → NE India. Intergrades with *arboreum* f. *roseum* and *arboreum* f. *album* which are generally placed here. Flowers red, pink or white.

R. arboreum ssp. *delavayi* In mixed forests and on forest margins. Often in open forests on rocky slopes of slate formation. Relatively drought resistant, 1200–3250m. Central Bhutan

RHODODENDRON ARBOREUM SSP. ZEYLANICUM in the mists of the Horton Plains National Park, Sri Lanka
COURTESY of www.sanchare.com

RHODODENDRON ARBOREUM SSP. ARBOREUM in the Phobjika Valley of Bhutan   DAVID SAYERS

R. ARBOREUM SSP. NILAGIRICUM at
Stronachullin Lodge, Argyll   HARTWIG SCHEPKER

→ NE India → SE Tibet → SW China → Burma (Myanmar) and Thailand. Intergrades with *R. arboreum* ssp. *arboreum* in Bhutan and NE India. Flowers blood-red, occasionally pink or white.

R. arboreum ssp. *delavayi* var. *peramoenum* In open mixed, sometimes dense, rain forest thickets and forest margins between 1600–3400m. NE India (Arunachal Pradesh) → W Yunnan. Flowers blood-red.

R. arboreum ssp. *delavayi* var. *albotomentosum* In dense rain forest, thickets and forest margins. Often clothed in epiphytes. 1600–3000m. West central Burma (Myanmar) and probably eastwards into Thailand. Flowers blood-red. Cultivated plants of this variety are invariably referable to what is listed as being *R. arboreum* ssp. *delavayi* Mount Victoria Form (Kingdon Ward 21976).

R. arboreum ssp. *nilagiricum* In upland mixed forests up to 2438m in the Nilgiri and Palni mountains of Tamil Nadu in the Western Ghats of S India. Flowers typically deep red but sometimes rose-pink and, rarely, white.

R. arboreum ssp. *zeylanicum* In upland forests of Sri Lanka up to the summit of Adam's Peak and other mountains. 900–2400m. Flowers deep red to rich pink. Differs from all other subspecies in its strongly bullate, very dark green leaves and its distinctive roughly textured bark.

Stitzer, Hoang and Hall (in *Rhododendron Species*, 2011, 89–99) add a new approach to the taxonomy of the species based on phylogeographic and DNA variations. They suggest that the three deep valley systems of W Yunnan may have acted to restrict gene flow between eastern and western populations, thus fostering the genetic split which can be observed between *R. arboreum* ssp. *arboreum* and ssp. *delavayi* groups. They further suggest that, following further research, ssp. *nilagiricum* and ssp. *zeylanicum* might be elevated to the rank of species.

CULTIVARS OF *RHODODENDRON ARBOREUM*

Being a species which possesses such a wide range of variation, it is inevitable that several forms of *Rhododendron arboreum* have been selected and named as being of particular horticultural merit; some have received awards.

How one actually evaluates one form from another is speculative and to better illustrate this point I will quote from a paragraph I wrote some 34 years ago (*Rhododendrons with Magnolias and Camellias*, 1978, 22) following a trek in central Nepal: '*A truly beautiful area on the eastern edge of the immense Kali Gandaki gorge, Daulagiri, Nilgiri and Annapurna high in the sky away to the north … . The myriad forms of* R. arboreum *run away as far as the eye could follow in a sea of pink, rose and scarlet – even the occasional splash of white. The thought of handing out AMs and FCCs along the ridge makes me smile. An RHS committee seems a world away and quite incomprehensible when one is so remotely situated and amidst such scenic majesty as this.*'

It sometimes happens that within a cline there occurs what can best be described as 'an acceleration point' where a species reaches its zenith. In my opinion the *R. arboreum* forests of central Nepal and those regions which run eastwards at least as far as Sikkim and perhaps into west Bhutan, constitute such a juncture. To the west and east of this central section of the Himalayas blood-red forms would seem to dominate and this characteristic continues to prevail in the easternmost ssp. and varieties as far as Thailand.

Be that as it may, in cultivation, gardeners, by their very nature, have selected certain clones and more than a few of these have received awards or other forms of registration.

Selected clones include:

R. arboreum 'Goat Fell' AM 1964. Registered by the National Trust for Scotland, Brodick Castle, Arran.

R. arboreum 'Rubaiyat' AM 1968. Registered by Edmund de Rothschild, Exbury Gardens, Hampshire.

Note: A staff member at Wakehurst Place, Sussex once inadvertently labelled this clone under the name 'Rubbermat' which could well have caused the Omar Khayyam to turn in his grave!

R. arboreum (ssp. *cinnamomeum*) f. *roseum* 'Tony Schilling' FCC 1974, AGM 1993. Registered by the Royal Botanic Gardens, Kew (Wakehurst Place).

Note: There is no evidence of ssp. *cinnamomeum* in the foliage of this clone, hence the brackets.

R. ARBOREUM 'GOAT FELL' at Lamellen, Cornwall
MIKE ROBINSON

RHODODENDRON ARBOREUM SSP. *ALBOTOMENTOSUM* 'ROBERT BARRY' at The San Francisco Botanical
Garden at Strybing Arboretum   ERIC HUNT

R. arboreum 'Fernhill Silver'. Registered by Mr S Walker and R Walker, 1985. Seedling raised by David Moore at Glasnevin Botanic Garden, Dublin in the 19th century. This is thought to have been raised from original Hooker seed sent direct to Moore from Kew. (Syn. 'Mrs E Darley') and grown at Fernhill, Co Dublin, Ireland.

R. arboreum 'Heligan'. Unknown registrant (pre 1996). Probably a gift from Sir Charles Lemon of Carclew, Cornwall who received material from J Hooker's original collections of 1848/9.

R. arboreum 'Alan Campbell-Johnson'. Registered by RE Thornton (2003). Raised from seed from collection made at Darjeeling, N India by the registrant.

R. arboreum 'Queen of Bhutan'. Registered by DW Goheen (1999). Selection from *R. arboreum* ssp. *cinnamomeum* collected in Bhutan.

R. arboreum 'Sir Edmund Hillary'. Registered by Heritage Park Rhododendron Charitable Trust (2010). From seed sent to New Zealand by the Queen of Nepal c1970.

R. arboreum 'Tiger's Nest'. Registered by High Beeches Conservation Trust (2008). From seed collected in west Bhutan above Paro by Anne and Edward Boscawen at 3048m.

R. arboreum ssp. *delavayi* var. *albotomentosum* 'Doctor Bowman'. Registered by C Tuomala (1984). Raised from KW21976.

R. arboreum ssp. *albotomentosum* 'Robert Barry'. Registrant unknown (pre 2011), California.

R. arboreum ssp. *nilagiricum* 'Tarun'. Registered by Girija Viraraghavan (1998). A white flowered selection from Mount Kudiakadu, Nilgiri Mountains, S India. Found by Tarun Chhabra and named by the registrant.

Windsor Great Park's holdings include an unregistered clone called 'Nancy Martin', which was named after Sir Eric Savill's cousin.

R. **'ENDSLEIGH PINK'** along the entrance drive to Endsleigh House, Devon
JULIE MCKENNA

HYBRIDISATION

When Joseph Hooker's 28 newly introduced species came in to cultivation, hybridisation accelerated dramatically, not least with the hardier forms of *Rhododendron arboreum*. When JR Gowen obtained flowering material of the low-altitude blood-red form from The Grange in Alresford and created *R.* 'Altaclarense' for the Earl of Carnarvon at Highclere perhaps the story began then. However, it soon became obvious that hardiness, or a lack of it, presented a problem, although crosses with hardy species such as *R. ponticum*, *R. catawbiense* and *R. maximum* did improve matters considerably. The 'blue tinge' caused by using these hardy species was another negative issue but when Hooker's harvests brought the higher altitude forms of *R. arboreum* (and its colour variants) and the scarlet of *R. thomsonii* and *R. barbatum* into the equation, the results improved extravagantly.

The use of *R. arboreum* during the last 185 years or so has been well recorded (WJ Bean et al) and does not require repeating here, indeed such has been its importance one might suggest an entire book could be written on the subject.

Suffice to state that old favourites such as *R.* 'Nobleanum', *R.* 'Broughtonii' and *R.* 'Russellianum' ('Cornish Early Red') all came about before Joseph Hooker's introductions but after 1849 things moved on apace with hybrids reaching the market from all manner of directions. Waterer's gave gardens gems such as *R.* 'Sir Robert Peel' and the evergreen favourite *R.* 'Pink Pearl' whilst Lee and Kennedy of Hammersmith produced *R.* 'Lee's Scarlet' early in the nineteenth century, preceded by van Houtte's *R.* 'Boddaertianum'.

RHODODENDRON 'BODDAERTIANUM'
SALLY HAYWARD

The late Lionel de Rothschild was of the opinion that *R. arboreum* was the *'single most important species in the story of hybridization as it gives colour to the hardiness of the rest.'*

The lists of hybrids are legion but allowing for the fact that everyone has their personal favourites perhaps I may be forgiven for listing a few of my own starting with the generally little planted *R.* 'Endsleigh Pink' which arose from the Endsleigh Estate, prior to 1917. This is almost definitely a cross between *R. arboreum* and *R. argyrophyllum* and exhibits the characteristics of both parents. Anyone who has driven down the approach road to the Endsleigh Hotel in west Devon in the spring cannot fail to be deeply impressed as it edges the road in mature extravagance.

Another I am virtually compelled to mention is the *arboreum* x *strigillosum* hybrid which bears my wife's maiden name – *R.* 'Victoria Hallett' (AM 1989). Raised by Giles Harold Loder in 1949/50 this early flowering clone was registered by High Beeches Conservation Trust in 1989 and, although precocious and frost tender, does well in sheltered woodland.

The utilisation of *R. arboreum* (and its several forms) has continued unabated both here and overseas. In the USA we have *R.* 'Mrs Jamie Frazer' registered by WA Dale (1991) and *R.* 'Bill Fee' from Singing Tree Garden and Nursery, registered in 2008. New Zealanders have produced *R.* 'Kaponga', raised by B Hollard, and R Gordon's widely acclaimed *R.* 'Rubicon', both registered in 1979. In Australia there is much to note, including *R.* 'Olinda Early Surprise' and *R.* 'Lighthouse' both registered by Van de Ven, in 1992 and 1995 respectively. In India, Viru Viraraghavan has been hybridising with *R. arboreum* ssp. *nilagiricum* to produce, among others, *R.* 'Palni Princess' (1999) and *R.* 'Palni Fire' (2010). The Kunming Botanic Garden has also recently registered *R.* 'Red Swoon' – a hybrid from *R. arboreum* spp. *delavayi*.

As a postscript it may be noted that *R.* 'Noyo Chief', once considered to be a form of *R. arboreum* ssp. *nilagiricum* is now recognised as being a hybrid of that subspecies, whilst *R.* 'Sir Charles Lemon' is accepted as being a natural hybrid between *R. arboreum* (ssp. *cinnamomeum*?) and *R. campanulatum*, ex Sir Joseph Hooker via Carclew, Cornwall.

RHODODENDRON 'VICTORIA HALLETT'
TONY SCHILLING

RHODODENDRON ARBOREUM – ITS ETHNIC, ECONOMIC AND CULTURAL CONNECTIONS

Unfortunate as it may be from the point of conservation, *Rhododendron arboreum* is highly regarded as a source of firewood in its native lands. This conservation concern is amplified by the fact that about 84% of energy consumed in Nepal comes from the use of firewood and this figure is probably echoed along the entire Himalayan chain. Not only is the species used for fuel it is also used by villagers to produce charcoal for sale to blacksmiths and goldsmiths.

Roxburgh stated that *'Captain Hardwicke informs us that the wood is in estimation among the natives for making gun stocks, or the stocks of their match-lock pieces.'*

The wood is also used to make household utensils, for building purposes, fencing, planking and furniture manufacture. It provides a long-lasting heat hence its extensive use as firewood.

Its ethnic benefits in Nepal are particularly well documented in *Plants and People of Nepal* (2002). The Nepalese hold the species in high esteem and in 1952 it was officially named as the country's national flower. The blossoms are said to be beneficial for curing sore throats and some ethnic groups pickle the flowers by mixing them with salt and chili (*Capsicum annuum*).

Flower petals are also dried and used as a tea but, from personal experience, I believe it to be an acquired taste! An extract from the bark is said to alleviate the symptoms of dysentery and a paste from the young leaves is used to relieve headaches. Immature foliage is used as a fish poison as well as a control for bed bugs. The young foliage is also said to be poisonous to cattle.

Understandably, the flowers are valued for personal adornment, as offerings in religious festivals or for sale in urban markets, especially in March when other flowers are scarce.

It is hardly surprising that *R. arboreum* has many different common names bestowed upon it by the equally numerous native groups who dwell within its trans-Himalayan forests. In the Garhwal of NW India we know from Captain Hardwicke's records that the locals give it the name 'boorons'. Nepal officially terms it 'laligurans', but each ethnic group

R. ARBOREUM SSP. DELAVAYI VAR. ALBOTOMENTOSUM KW21976
at Stronachullin Lodge, Argyll   HARTWIG SCHEPKER

within the country has its own particular name for the plant.

Further along in Bhutan it is termed 'Ito Metog' in the country's official language of Dzong kha, whereas travelling eastwards where the Shachop dialect prevails, it is known as 'Zhu-dang Metog'.

In China, where the subspecies *delavayi* occurs, it is known (in Mandarin) as 'May Ying Dù Juān' and in Chinese Tibet as 'Ya Zhou Mian Dùjuān'. In some parts of China it is utilised as a hedging plant rather like British gardeners sometimes use *R. ponticum*.

In the southern Indian state of Tamil Nadu the Toda tribals (an ancient pastoral people) of the Nilgiri mountains use the name 'pershk' for the subspecies *nilagiricum*. Many hamlets are proud of ancient sacred rhododendron trees which grow close to their homes, and priests even have specific prayer names for individual specimens. Doors of temples are frequently fashioned out of the timber and the tree is used in their rituals especially in wedding and pregnancy ceremonies. The rhododendron is often mentioned in Toda songs both traditional and contemporary, and honey made from its nectar is said to be of exceptional flavour (Viraraghavan, *pers comm*).

R. ARBOREUM SSP. CINNAMOMEUM – the 11m tall, white-flowered form at Trewithen   GARY LONG

STATURE OF *RHODODENDRON ARBOREUM* IN GREAT BRITAIN AND IRELAND

Very large specimens of *Rhododendron arboreum* are to be found in many of the early estates, these venerable individuals being usually found in areas of high rainfall, high humidity and relatively mild winters. There can be few, if any, of the great woodland gardens of the English Westcountry, Western Scotland or the renowned estates of Ireland that do not possess at least one good specimen.

One of the best known sites for Hooker's original introductions is Stonefield Castle Hotel in Argyll and Bute. Specimens there are now more than 160 years old and, although not champion examples of their kind, they have reached very impressive proportions. There are other fine trees at nearby Kilmory Castle and still more, further south at Castle Kennedy in Dumfries and Galloway, not forgetting those in the balmy climes of Cornwall or Ireland.

Recent records indicate that Castle Kennedy and Mount Stewart, Greyabbey in County Down, jointly possess the tallest specimens in these Isles, both reaching to 16m although the Scottish tree has the greatest girth at 1.72m. This figure pales into insignificance when compared to the specimen at Mount Stuart on the Isle of Bute which currently measures 2.47m– its height being a mere 10m is far less inspiring.

The champion specimen of *R. arboreum* ssp. *cinnamomeum* stands 13m tall at Castle Kennedy and very probably dates back to Hooker's original introductions.

Several examples of *R. arboreum* f. *album* can be found on the approach drive to Kilmory Castle – again traceable to Hooker. Two of these have a matching height of 9m. Further south at Muncaster Castle in Cumbria can be found a 12m tall example of *R. arboreum* f. *roseum*, the tallest yet recorded.

Wales has a tree of *R. arboreum* measuring 12m in height growing at Clyne Gardens, Black Pill, Glamorganshire, but the country may well possess others as yet unrecorded.

Cornwall's champion is said to be one at Burncoose measuring 14m in height. Trewithen, in the same county, possesses at least two fine examples of *R. arboreum*, one at 9m and the other at 11m.

RHODODENDRON ARBOREUM **FOREST** near Tarapani, Central Nepal   GREG WILLIS

Some subspecies of *R. arboreum* have generally proved to be too tender for all but the mildest gardens. This fact applies especially to ssp. *nilagiricum* and ssp. *delavayi* var. *peramoenum* which in all probability will only succeed under glass. Subspecies *delavayi* var. *albotomentosum* (ex Mount Victoria, Burma) KW21976 has shown a little more promise in Britain. To date it is surviving in the Perthshire garden of Peter Cox and until relatively recently grew to a height of some 3m at Wakehurst Place in Sussex before succumbing to a severe winter. A magnificent example is to be found at Stronachullin Lodge, raised from Kingdon Ward seed collected in 1956 from Mount Victoria in Burma.

Perhaps the most interesting records relate to ssp. *zeylanicum*. Although several good examples of this relatively tender plant can be found in various Scottish gardens including Inverewe, Stonefield Castle Hotel and Logan Botanic Garden, the finest of all is at Arduaine near Oban. When last measured in 1991 it stood multi-stemmed at 9m in height. Reliable records tell of material being sent from the hills of Sri Lanka to Britain in a tea chest.

The *R. arboreum* 'Fernhill Silver' at Sandyford, County Down is currently over 13.5m tall, while the clone of f. *roseum* 'Tony Schilling' at Wakehurst Place is over 9m in height. Exbury Gardens in Hampshire, from whence the clone 'Rubaiyat' originated can boast of at least 21 specimens of this selection, the finest being almost 6m tall in 2011. The natural hybrid *R*. 'Sir Charles Lemon' is best admired at Castle Kennedy which has a tree of 14m. At this stature it must surely be from Hooker's 1848/9 introductions.

STATURE OF *RHODODENDRON ARBOREUM* IN THE WILD

The fact that in its native haunts *Rhododendron arboreum* grows to a great stature is well known, but individual records add substance to the reality.

Peter Cox has written of finding enormous trees of *R. arboreum* ssp. *delavayi* var. *peramoenum* in the Salween region of Yunnan (*Rhododendrons with Camellias and Magnolias* 1999, 46–7). There he recorded specimens in excess of 25m. Although these were in a sheltered gully, and therefore drawn up by the surrounding forest, this height is by no means unique.

During the spring of 1983, whilst botanising on the flanks of the Gurkha Himalaya in Central Nepal, I had the privilege of passing through relatively untouched forests of *R. arboreum* which were especially rich in their variety of colour – but it was their stature which was particularly impressive. Never during my three years of exploring within the Asian forests had I seen finer examples which in this instance reached heights of 25m or more. Not just a few exceptional ligneous leviathans, but in near-uniform groves of multi-stemmed magnificence. One of these superb trees registered a girth of some 4.5m. Surely there, in the hills above the Dorandi Khola, where this species arguably reaches its meridian, these noble groves deserve official protection of some sort?

In 1938 Frank S Smythe wrote *The Valley of Flowers* (realistically referred to as the Bhyundar Valley). Smythe was of course in the Garhwal Himalaya and, as well as being a mountaineer of international fame, was also an inspired writer and a gardener. Whilst en route to revisit his beloved valley, he paused to rest above the village of Dungri and later wrote in his magnum opus *'The forest was profoundly silent … not even in the Sikkim forests have I seen finer tree rhododendrons, and there was one moss-clad giant which cannot have been less than 5ft in diameter. For how many centuries had these trees endured? Long before the wooden ships of 'The Company' sailed to India they must have established themselves on the knees of the Himalayas.'*

It is perhaps appropriate for these notes to run full circle and end where they began, in the hills of NW India. When Captain Hardwicke first came upon *Rhododendron arboreum* in the spring of 1796 the story of this far flung species fired the imagination of botanists and gardeners alike. Even today, some 215 years later, we remain captivated by its arboreal grandeur.

ACKNOWLEDGEMENTS

I wish to thank the following for their help in the writing of this article:

John Anderson, Chris Brickell, David Cooke, Peter Cox, Mark Flanagan, Martin Gardner, Andrew Jackson, Dr Alan Leslie, Christopher Loder, Brian Mathew, Julie McKenna, David Sayers, Victoria Schilling, The Tree Register of the British Isles, Viru Viraraghavan and Dr Mark Watson.

I am especially grateful for Pam Hayward's guidance, advice and assistance, without which my task would have been considerably harder.

Tony Schilling VMH

was Curator of Wakehurst Place, Sussex from 1967–1991 and now delights in gardening amidst the majestic mountain landscape of northwest Scotland

SELECTED REFERENCES ■ Allen, C. *A Mountain in Tibet,* André Deutsch (1982). Anon. GH Cave, an obituary, *Kew Guild Journal,* (1966). Bean, WJ. *Trees and Shrubs Hardy in the British Isles* Vol III, 598, John Murray (Eighth Edition) (1976). Chamberlain, DF. *Notes from the Royal Botanic Garden Edinburgh,* 39.2 (1982). Cox, K et al. *Riddle of the Tsangpo Gorges,* Antique Collectors' Club (2001). Cox, PA. *The Larger Rhododendron Species,* Batsford, London (1990). Cox, PA and Cox, KNE. *Encyclopedia of Rhododendron Hybrids,* Batsford (1988). Davidian, D. *The Rhododendron Species* Vol II, Batsford, London (1989). Desmond, R. *Sir Joseph Dalton Hooker,* Antique Collectors' Club (1999). Forrest, M. In *The Rhododendron Story* (Ed Cynthia Postan), Royal Horticultural Society (1996). Grierson, AJC and Long, DG. *Flora of Bhutan,* 2.1, RBG Edinburgh (1991). Kneller, M. *The Book of Rhododendrons,* David and Charles (1995). Lang, D. In *Quarterly Bulletin of the Alpine Garden Society,* 59.3, (1991). Leach, D. The Discovery of Rhododendrons on Jamaica, *Journal of American Rhododendron Society,* 11.3,(1957). Manandhar, NP. *Plants and People of Nepal,* Timber Press (2002). Smythe, FS. *The Valley of Flowers,* Hodder and Stoughton (1938).

Magnolia grandiflora, a noble species with a complementary court of cultivars

KEVIN PARRIS

***MAGNOLIA GRANDIFLORA* 'BRACKEN'S BROWN BEAUTY'** encircles a fountain to create an outdoor room at the end of the Allée at the Milliken Arboretum on Milliken's Corporate Campus in Spartanburg, SC   KEVIN PARRIS

WHEN YOU ARE RAISED in the southeastern United States, you take many simple pleasures for granted. Sweet iced tea, homemade peach ice cream (made with fresh peaches of course), fried apple pie, and Southern Magnolia are just a few things in which I assumed everyone on earth could readily indulge.

The end of the innocence for me came sometime in my teen years when I learned that sweet tea was not a standard menu item north of the Mason-Dixon Line and many poor souls had never tasted a fresh peach. I was also surprised to learn that only my grandmother knew how to make a 'real' fried apple pie, and Southern Magnolia was a not a common tree in every neighborhood across the land. Even more stunning were the revelations that some people preferred their apple pie to be prepared differently and others had the audacity to say that Southern Magnolia is just a gangly, cumbersome, mess of a tree. Sacrilege.

NATURAL GROVE OF *MAGNOLIA GRANDIFLORA*, Beech Island, SC
JENKS FARMER

granted. Ironically, when I travelled to China in 2009 for the International Symposium on the Family *Magnoliaceae*, I learned that *M. grandiflora* is truly revered on the other side on the earth. The species was heavily represented in botanical gardens, and more surprisingly, it was a street tree in Guangzhou and Kunming. Stunning silk replicas even graced the interior of Shanghai Airport. So, despite having to alter my food choices for the two week visit, there were some comforting images of home. I came away from that trip, my first international journey, with the sense that *M. grandiflora* is one of the most highly respected tree species around the globe. The nobility of this species has allowed it to accompany the architecture of actual castles, and what we might perceive as modern day castles.

Although scores of *M. grandiflora* cultivars have been in the trade since the species was introduced to cultivation, their availability has

Magnolia grandiflora, known as Southern Magnolia or Bull Bay is indigenous to coastal regions of states that border the southern Atlantic Ocean and the Gulf of Mexico. Since entering cultivation in the mid-eighteenth century it has naturalized, greatly extending the range of the species, allowing for numerous cultivar selections to be made.

M. grandiflora is a hexaploid species ($2n=6x=114$), giving it a rich genetic complement and a host of diverse traits that may be expressed, depending on natural selection from environmental pressure, or human selection for ornamental attributes. It is no wonder this species in now heavily cultivated on every continent of the world except Antarctica.

In fact, we can speculate that mankind has significantly repaired the loss of natural range and greatly expanded the area which this species enjoyed prior to glaciation.

In my part of the world many people take this species and the value of its diverse traits for

A MAGNIFICENT *MAGNOLIA GRANDIFLORA* graces 'a modern castle':
Old Main at Wofford College, Spartanburg, SC   KEVIN PARRIS

MAGNOLIA GRANDIFLORA shows itself to be a fine
urban tree in the Yunnan province   KEVIN PARRIS

(soil profile desiccation) and associated foot traffic (soil compaction). This stress in turn causes the tree to defoliate more noticeably, with increased frequency. For the magnoli-aphile the messy tendencies are a trivial distraction to the foliage, flowers and form of a grand specimen, but the gardening public can be less forgiving. As such, prudent cultivar selection is a must. A decade into the 21st century, we have many from which to choose, and waiting in the wings is the promise of plenty more.

In Dorothy Callaway's superlative 1994 publication *The World of Magnolias*, 73 cultivars of *M. grandiflora* are listed. Dr Michael Dirr includes descriptions of 88 cultivars in the sixth edition (2009) of his *Manual of Woody Landscape Plants*. There is some overlap, but between these two publications over 100 distinct cultivars are mentioned. Many of those mentioned in both publications represent the most well-known and respected selections. I strongly recommend that anyone with more than a modest interest in *M. grandiflora* consult both texts for a glance at these extensive cultivar listings.

typically had a local focus. Relatively few selections are widely distributed outside their region of commercial origin. This seems to be based partially on climatic adaptability, but familiarity of name due to the influence of marketing is a significant factor. Having been a landscape designer I know how easy it is to slip into a routine of specifying what the local nursery typically offers. Customers often demand a streamlined project over one that explores the inventory of a myriad of sources. Hastily executed selection of a *M. grandiflora* cultivar for a particular landscape is what leads to most of the negative opinions that people have of this noble tree. The complaint most often voiced is that the trees are 'messy' when they gradually shed foliage during the spring and hot, dry summer months as new foliage and flowers win the battle for allocation of carbohydrates. The second common dislike is the overall size of the tree, which leads to the removal of the lower canopy for improved visibility and pedestrian access. This removal of lower canopy has unintended consequences – it leads to increased light and air movement

MAGNOLIA GRANDIFLORA complements the
ancient walls of Leeds Castle, Kent   EMILY WELCH

THE LARGEST *M. GRANDIFLORA* IN SE FRANCE
(32m tall, 4.4m girth and 150 years old)

THIERRY LAMANT

A goal of this article is to put some of these cultivars into context by dividing them into three categories:

Classics: These selections have been in cultivation for more than 25 years and still enjoy frequent use.

Oldies but Goodies: Cultivars that still have significant merit, but have not maintained widespread popularity. (Individual readers may wish to interchange some of the selections in the 'Classics' and 'Oldies but Goodies' categories. I have simply attempted to best communicate current trends from the perspective of someone living within the natural range of this species.)

New Releases: Selections which have been made in the last 25 years. I cannot begin to discuss all cultivars and will attempt to simply highlight a range of selections that illustrate the diversity of worthy traits that are manifested in this species.

The conclusion of this article will take a look at recent hybridization efforts with *M. grandiflora*, because these efforts may yield the most exciting cultivar introductions in years to come.

CLASSICS

M. **'Claudia Wannamaker'** Introduced by John F Brailsford Sr, of Shady Grove Nursery in Orangeburg, SC, this cultivar was the first to become readily available in the southeastern US. From my perspective it still embodies a nearly perfect mixture of traits that make it fit for use in the modern landscape. Claudia develops into a relatively compact tree, while maintaining a nice horizontal drapery of branches. Many of the newer cultivars selected for compact habit have upward sweeping laterals that brandish the lower leaf surface. I have learned from my experiences as a garden designer that while I see *M. grandiflora* foliage with deep indumentum prominently displayed as an attribute, this trait is not preferred by all discerning gardeners. Claudia has enough indumentum to provide color contrast to the upper leaf surface, without being 'too fuzzy' for some. The flower is not large by *M. grandiflora* standards, but is nicely proportionate to the foliage. So, in regard to size, habit, foliage, and flower qualities, Claudia is a nice 'happy medium' and will always deserve a place in gardens. A sheared hedge of 'Claudia' has been maintained for approximately 30 years at the Milliken Arboretum in Spartanburg, SC, a testimony to the flexibility of landscape use that this cultivar, and others possess.

M. **'Bracken's Brown Beauty'** Since being selected as a four year old seedling in a field in Piedmont, SC by Ray Bracken, this has become a standard by which other cultivars are often judged, especially in the eastern US. Landscapes in upstate South Carolina are a virtual monoculture of this cultivar because of availability, dependability, and aesthetic quality. Exceptional cold hardiness has allowed 'Bracken's' to experience widespread popularity. The most effective planting of this cultivar that I have observed is where it is used to create an outdoor room for a fountain at the end of the Allée at Milliken Arboretum.

M. **'Little Gem'** A true gem that has allowed *M. grandiflora* to find its way into many gardens that otherwise would be too small to accommodate the dimensions typical of the species. Found by Warren Steed in Candor, NC, *M.* 'Little Gem' became known throughout the US, and later worldwide, largely because of the

***MAGNOLIA GRANDIFLORA* 'LITTLE GEM'** (*TOP*) displays its versatility in this beautiful espaliered arch, and
***M. GRANDIFLORA* 'CLAUDIA WANNAMAKER'** (*BOTTOM*) is maintained as a finely clipped hedge at the
Milliken Arboretum in Spartanburg, SC   KEVIN PARRIS

production and demand created by Monrovia Nursery Co., Azusa California. Despite being one of the more difficult cultivars to propagate by cuttings, the popularity of *M.* 'Little Gem' forced growers to refine their techniques to meet the demand. In the southeastern US, *M.* 'Little Gem' is quite remontant (flowering more than once in a season) with flowers being produced here in the months of May–November. The flowers are small by *M. grandiflora* standards, but proportionate to the foliage, and abundantly produced. The heavy flower production, coupled with the subsequent fruit development and drain on carbohydrates keeps the growth rate in check. Perhaps the only ornamental flaw of *M.* 'Little Gem' is a branch structure that lacks a strong central leader. The thin branches terminated by dense whorls of foliage predispose trees to damage from accumulation of snow and ice. In my garden the top half of my plant snapped off during a winter ice storm, but I was able to re-establish a leader, suppress lateral branch development and mold a tightly columnar specimen that anchors the corner of my home. The ability of *M.* 'Little Gem' to adapt to frequent pruning is most clearly displayed in an espaliered specimen at Milliken Arboretum.

M. **'D.D. Blanchard'** This is certainly one of the most striking cultivars in widespread commercial production. The bold, reddish-brown backed foliage and robust form set *M.* 'D.D. Blanchard' apart from the pack. Although it does not flower as a small tree, and may produce a sparse display on established specimens, this cultivar still deserves the widespread popularity it has gained. Flowers are not required to earn merit for this selection. I am greeted each morning I drive onto campus by a grouping of *M.* 'D.D. Blanchard' set against an adjacent specimen of *Cedrus deodara* 'Bracken's Select'. The color and textural contrast is as dramatic as can be obtained without the presence of flowers. But, as striking as the foliage is, it can also be detrimental to the tree, as it can retain damaging accumulations of snow and ice. It is probably best used in a climate with infrequent winter precipitation.

M. **'Edith Bogue'** One of the more hardy cultivars, 'Edith' provides an opportunity for many gardeners to experience *M. grandiflora* that otherwise would not be able to cultivate the species. For many of us this exceptional cold hardiness is not necessary, and there are more attractive cultivars than 'Edith', but she deserves high merit due to an interesting observation

MAGNOLIA GRANDIFLORA **'D.D. BLANCHARD'** (*LEFT*) at Swarthmore College, PA and close-up (*RIGHT*) at Spartanburg Community College, SC   KEVIN PARRIS

THE NARROW GROWTH HABIT OF *MAGNOLIA GRANDIFLORA* **'HASSE'** used to great effect at the Wofford
College Gymnasium, Spartanburg, SC   KEVIN PARRIS

that has been made by Douglas Justice with the
University of British Columbia Botanical Garden
in Vancouver, Canada. He notes 'Magnolia
grandiflora *does not always succeed in the Vancouver
area, primarily because we lack the quick-warming
soils and sustained summer heat and moisture
required to fuel its growth. The area's climatic
limitations can cause plants that are not selected for
specific tolerances to either languish or fall to pieces.
For example, the early and long cold winter of
2010/2011 was exceptionally hard on many M.*
grandiflora *seedlings, and in particular, two well-
known cultivars: 'D.D. Blanchard' and 'Little Gem'.
Most specimens of these cultivars were not only
broken up by the early wet snow, but were ultimately
killed by the cold. The following commonly available
cultivars are known to perform reasonably well in
the Vancouver area. All have glossy, dark green leaves
and creamy white, bowl-shaped flowers, and leaves
that are covered below in dense orangey hairs. 'Edith
Bogue' is probably the cold-hardiest M.* grandiflora
in commerce.' Bob Head of Head Ornamentals in
Seneca, SC, has also made an observation about
rooted cuttings and small container stock in his

nursery. In his experience in USDA climate Zone
7, in the foothills of the Blue Ridge Mountains,
the root system of *M. grandiflora* typically dies
around the outer edge of the container after
exposure to winter conditions. 'Edith' is the
only cultivar that reliably maintains healthy
white root tips adjacent to the container after
this exposure, while other cultivars have to
regenerate roots from insulated tissue within the
root ball. This could be an indication that 'Edith'
more efficiently translocates and stores
carbohydrates in root tissue in preparation for
dormancy. Should we seek to introgress this trait
into new *M. grandiflora* introductions? If I lived
in colder climate, I would have already initiated
this endeavor.

M. 'Hasse' Another introduction from John F
Brailsford Sr, of Shady Grove Nursery, and
probably the most distinctive one covered here
due to the tightly columnar growth habit.
Flower production is modest, but if you have a
narrow space and need a striking broad-leaved
evergreen tree, this is it. With just a little
diligent pruning this cultivar can add a

M. GRANDIFLORA 'HASSE' also makes a perfect free-standing accent plant   KEVIN PARRIS

dramatic flair to the narrowest of planting spaces. The planting along the gymnasium at Wofford College in Spartanburg, SC, nicely illustrates this. M. 'Hasse' does have a couple of flaws that surface in production. It is one of the more stubborn to propagate by cuttings, and is difficult to successfully transplant from the field. Fall transplants in the southeastern US often die back partially during the first winter and need to have a central leader re-established over the next couple of growing seasons. It is a worthy cultivar nonetheless, as well placed specimens ultimately require little attention to stay in bounds.

OLDIES BUT GOODIES:

M. 'Saint Mary' Selected by the Glen St Mary Nursery of Florida prior to 1930, this cultivar has been distributed worldwide and still has some regional popularity in the United States. Gary Knox of the University of Florida reports that it remains one of his favorites. It is also reported to be one of the more widely produced cultivars in Australia, though newer selections are beginning to edge ahead. Like M. 'Claudia Wannamaker' this selection embodies refined 'typical' characteristics of Southern Magnolia with foliage of considerable substance. When compared to the foliage of M. 'Little Gem' the texture difference between the cultivars is quite pronounced.

M. 'Samuel Sommer' The first time I viewed a specimen of this cultivar was at the San Francisco Botanic Garden, which is a haven for many magnolias. I was impressed by the substance of its foliage and the way it grabbed my attention as I made my way through the garden. The leaves are larger and the plant is more bulky than M. 'Claudia Wannamaker' and M. 'Little Gem', but I would like to suggest that this cultivar is a better choice for large scale landscapes where substance and coarse texture are needed to slow down the eye of a hurried passerby. Richard Figlar notes that the flowers often have 12 tepals. The gardener who is keenly focused on floral characters will likely prefer this selection to mass market cultivars like M. 'Little Gem'. Ornamental fruiting qualities are often overlooked in this species but Pat McCracken, plantsman and magnolia expert, Zebulon, NC, points out that the consistently ruby-tinted aggregates of follicles on M. 'Samuel Sommer' are hard to ignore.

M. GRANDIFLORA **GREENBACK™** has glossy foliage which reflects light into a landscape   KEVIN PARRIS

M. 'Exmouth' This is an exceptional selection with flowers that vary from the typical 9 tepaled form, to those which are fully double. This is still one of the more common cultivars in England and Australia, but it has never caught hold in the United States. I believe that if more people could see this tree in flower it would garner more attention in the US market.

M. 'Majestic Beauty' Monrovia Nursery originally released this cultivar that at one time was the most widely available selection in the United States. The comment above about *M.* 'Samuel Sommer' regarding the importance of substance and texture in large scale landscapes applies here as well. All too often it seems that pretty and petite wins out over gorgeous and grand. You can say what you want about immense producers of plants and the sometimes unfair influence of marketing to the masses, but Monrovia and *M.* 'Majestic Beauty' blazed a trail by raising the standard for what the public should expect from a nursery produced *M. grandiflora.*

NEW RELEASES

'MGTIG' PP#9243, **Greenback™** I first saw Greenback™ while touring Bold Spring Nursery back in 1991. This John Barbour introduction is the polar opposite of 'D.D. Blanchard', and seeing them positioned together in retail nurseries likely leads an average consumer to believe they must be different species. Greenback™ forms a densely structured framework of branches as a young container grown specimen. The glossy, convex leaves are positioned in a manner that the polished surface cannot be ignored. The tight habit allows it to hold form without much structural pruning as a young tree. Greenback™ has been used effectively as backdrop for the garden outside the Gibbs Cancer Center at Spartanburg Regional Medical Center, completely masking the presence of an adjacent parking area. I have observed decline of the central leader resulting from diminished water uptake on field grown transplants during the first winter, so container

STUNNING YOUNG TREES OF *M. GRANDIFLORA* **ALTA™** demonstrate the ornamental versatility of this species   COURTESY OF PLANTIPP

production is best for this selection to avoid root loss during transplanting.

'TMGH' PP#11612, **Alta™** This is a seedling selection from *M.* 'Hasse' which maintains a narrowly conical habit in youth and ultimately broadens with age. The foliage is narrow and quite distinctive in the manner that is positioned tightly along the branches. Flowering is limited on young specimens, but this should not be a deterrent for using it, as the density makes it ideal for a large evergreen screen. Flower production is simply a bonus. Although Alta™ has not held to narrow habit long term, it would certainly be adaptable to selective pruning, or occasional shearing that would help it hold a more streamlined form for decades.

'Southern Charm' PP#13049, **Teddy Bear™** An introduction from Bob Head of Head Ornamentals in Seneca, SC. Teddy Bear™ gets the award for the cultivar with the best name. It is an impressive tree in youth and makes a very recognizable specimen as it obtains size. The leaves are as round as any *M. grandiflora*, extremely dark, glossy and nicely positioned along stout branches. Slow growth and heavy brown indumentum keep it huggable like a teddy bear for quite a few years. Much like Alta™, flower production can be sparse, but despite this, I prefer this selection to *M.* 'Little Gem' for a small property where a singular specimen with character is required.

'STRgra' PP# 13851, **Baby Grand™** An introduction from Australia that is truly dwarf. I have only recently acquired an accession of this plant for evaluation, but am optimistic about the commercial potential. Flower buds are present on my 12 inches high by 18 inches wide plant and the rounded habit which is reported is becoming evident. Reports indicate the mature size will be approximately 10 feet and recommended spacing for groupings or hedges is 5 to 7 feet. The foliage is more refined than previous compact introductions such as *M.* 'Harold Poole'. In the southeastern US *M. grandiflora* is not thought of as a subject for formal or semi-formal hedging, but this introduction may begin to change that mindset. I can easily envision this plant taking the place of *Ligustrum japonicum* in well-designed gardens. Baby Grand™ has a healthy marketing effort behind it that could keep it

M. GRANDIFLORA **TEDDY BEAR™** is compact and shapely with superb foliage and indumentum
KEVIN PARRIS

around for a mention in the classics category one day if it lends itself to the typical climactic range of the species.

M. **'Kay Parris'** I humbly round out the new releases with a cultivar that wasn't 'released' in the official sense. It has, however, amazingly 'emerged' onto the scene. Kay Parris was my mother, and I named this selection as a tribute to her. As a naive 24 year old horticulturist I planted seed from *M.* 'Little Gem' with the intent of putting her name on a plant I could use in local landscapes and give to friends and family members. Twenty years later I can proudly report that is now being grown by an increasing number of nurseries in the eastern US. I have read reports about it being distributed in England and Belgium. The greatest quantity produced any-where is likely in Australia where Coolwyn Nurseries has become the center of distribution on that continent. The attributes include narrow, wavy foliage with heavy brown indumentum, and remontant flowering that often occurs in the first year of production. As new growth develops the vegetative buds are

AN ESPALIERED *M. GRANDIFLORA* 'KAY PARRIS' at Bartlett Arboretum in Charlotte, NC displays the potential of this cultivar for the smaller garden   GREG PAIGE

subtended by reddish-pink stipules which are striking in a sunny location. Propagation began in 1993 at Gilbert's Nursery in Chesnee, South Carolina when the original specimen produced four flowers only 24 months after the seed was sown. The first specimens were planted in trial sites in South Carolina, North Carolina, and Georgia in 1994–1995 and have reached 25–30 feet tall with a width of 10–12 feet. 'Kay' has performed well in New York, New Jersey, and Pennsylvania, displaying unexpected cold hardiness. Pat McCracken is the individual most responsible for initiating widespread interest in 'Kay', for which I am immensely grateful. In 2010 I was given the opportunity to tell the story of this plant in the *Journal of the Magnolia Society International.* Needless to say, it is my favorite cultivar.

THE FUTURE

For the avid magnoliaphile, and maybe even a large contingent of casual gardeners, *Magnolia grandiflora* represents the best of the best. It is a noble, long-lived species that etches the framework of some of the world's most endearing places and complements grandiose architecture. Personally witnes-sing the emergence of a cul-tivated plant selection has been

M. GRANDIFLORA 'KAY PARRIS' foliage surfaces and flowers provide a stark contrast to one another in this bouquet   KEVIN PARRIS

an inspiring journey which undoubtedly fueled my interest in this amazing plant species. Ultimately I suspect the recent popularity that *M*. 'Kay Parris' has gained will begin to fade, just like the 'oldies but goodies' in this article, but, it could also become a classic. Only time will tell. The following was conveyed to me by John Allman from Nurseries Online of Australia, www.nurseriesonline.com.au. It basically illustrates how the gardening public is interested in what is new and heavily marketed. John reports that *M*. 'Little Gem' is by far the biggest seller in Australia, historically followed by *M*. 'Exmouth', *M*. 'Saint Mary', and Greenback™. This year he anticipates that *M*. 'Little Gem' will remain on top, but *M*. 'Kay Parris' and Teddy Bear™ will top *M*. 'Exmouth' and *M*. 'Saint Mary' after only a few years of presence in the market. By comparison, *M*. 'Kay Parris', which was never patented in the U.S., and Teddy Bear™ have less demand in upstate South Carolina, where they originated, and still struggle a bit for name recognition when compared to classics like *M*. 'Little Gem', *M*. 'Bracken's Brown Beauty' and *M*. 'Claudia Wannamaker'.

What will the world of *M. grandiflora* look like in another 10 years, or 20 years? Bill Smith of Richmond, Virginia and others have developed intraspecific hybrids using some of best cultivars mentioned above. Most seedlings of

M. GRANDIFLORA 'KAY PARRIS' is also splendid for en masse planting, seen here at Spartanburg Community College, SC   KEVIN PARRIS

M. 'Kay Parris' that I have observed look as impressive as the original did 20 years ago. In a landscape or nursery full of cultivars with refined ornamental characteristics, there is potential in every seed. Pat McCracken has been keenly aware of this for almost 30 years. He believes the tip of the iceberg has only been found in regard to the variation and combination of traits that could arise within this species. The quest for a *M. grandiflora* with pink flowers has long been discussed. It has been a dream that many breeders have pondered. But introgression of color into this white flowered species will be difficult because *M. grandiflora* is hexaploid, with the chromosome content 2n=6x=114, compared to diploid, 2n=2x=38 of any known reproductively compatible species that exhibits pink or red tepal coloration. F1 interspecific hybrids always favor *M. grandiflora* because of the 3:1 ratio. Let us take a look at hybridization as we consider the future.

INTRASPECIFIC HYBRIDS

While all cultivars of *Magnolia grandiflora* are technically intraspecific hybrids, documentation of selections originating from controlled crosses between currently established cultivars is sparse. *M*. 'Kay Parris' is a putative hybrid of 'Little Gem' x 'Bracken's Brown Beauty', but we can't be certain. Other popular cultivars also have the maternal parent identified (eg Alta™ from *M*. 'Hasse'), but a vast majority are chance seedlings that matured with graceful grandeur under the watchful eye of a gardener or nurseryman. While it is difficult to imagine that there is still room for improvement of this species, Bill Smith of Richmond, Virginia has been working to make additional refinements. I have germinated plants acquired through the International Magnolia Society's Seed Counter from Bill's cross of 'Southern Charm' Teddy Bear™ x 'Kay Parris'. One accession displays obovate foliage similar to the maternal parent while flowering precociously 24 months after

THE 'FREEMAN HYBRID' MAGNOLIAS at the US National Arboretum   KEVIN PARRIS

germination, reminiscent of the pollen parent. Witnessing such refinement of traits in seedling progeny due to selection for ornamental attributes by mankind causes me to ponder the future for the species. In my community, which is certainly mirrored by many others, we have scattered naturalized populations of Southern Magnolia among the mixed hardwood and pine forests that border developments and roadways. These are the bird distributed offspring of older seed produced specimens planted by previous generations on residential and commercial property. Most of these populations contain nondescript individuals that lack the merit of a cultivar with character. Compared to a generation ago, today's landscapes are heavily loaded with a litany of cultivars. As birds distribute this seed to the natural spaces that border our urban centers, we are clearly redirecting the natural selection taking place in the species. It would not be a far-fetched notion to consider the possibility in 30 more years that 50–75 percent of all *Magnolia grandiflora* 'naturally' occurring around the perimeter of communities I frequent will be the offspring of *M.* 'Little Gem' or *M.* 'Bracken's Brown Beauty', since that is what is still planted

heavily, along with maturing specimens of the same. Now consider this: in selecting for ornamental qualities we typically desire precocious and remontant flowers. Progeny of modern cultivars are more likely to bloom early and often. Subsequent populations that arise will reach reproductive maturity more quickly, with more abundant seed production. We have, in essence, 'jump started' the ability of this already genetically rich species to adapt and more successfully naturalize. The following gives us even more to consider.

INTERSPECIFIC HYBRIDS

M. **'Maryland'** (*grandiflora* × *virginiana*) An original 'Freeman Hybrid' developed by Oliver Freeman of the US National Arboretum. It was the only one of several reported 'Freeman Hybrids' to be confirmed as a tetraploid (2n=4x=76) by flow cytometry. *M.* 'Griffin' and *M.* 'Sweet Summer' have the relative genome size of a hexaploid which indicates they are entirely *M. grandiflora*. *M.* 'Maryland' and future confirmed tetraploid selections are potentially important for breeding because of their reduced chromosome count, allowing for more balanced

MAGNOLIA 'MARYLAND' has wonderful foliage inherited from
M. grandiflora and a tendency not to open its blooms fully

RICHARD FIGLAR

cultivars. They all have foliage that strongly resembles *M. grandiflora*, but the red stamens of *M. sieboldii* have been displayed in several of the progeny that have flowered.

These hybrids are important because *M. sieboldii* is a precociously flowering species and the chromosome content in this hybrid is reduced to 2n=4x=76 for future crosses.

insignis MGA 355 × *grandiflora* 'Kay Parris' A breakthrough that demonstrates *M. grandiflora* can be successfully crossed with species from section Manglietia. This hybrid was developed at Magnolian Grove Arboretum, the garden of Dick and Anita Figlar, from a controlled cross that was performed in May 2008. Tetraploid genome size has been confirmed by flow cytometry. It brings hope to the prospect of successfully hybridizing *M. grandiflora* with larger flowered, pink/red tepaled species like *M. garrettii* and *M. grandis*.

introgression of traits from diploid parental species in future crosses.

'Maryland' × *grandiflora* An interesting seedling of *M.* 'Maryland' which germinated at Magnolian Grove Arboretum under the watchful eye of Dick Figlar. Verified by flow cytometry as a pentaploid (2n=5x=95), this specimen reveals that *M.* 'Maryland' was open pollinated by one of the *M. grandiflora* nearby.

(*grandiflora*×*virginiana*) × *virginiana* The identity of this sample from a specimen at the US National Arboretum collected by Research Geneticist, Richard Olsen, was verified as a triploid (2n=3x=57) by flow cytometry, indicating a backcross to *M. virginiana*. It is not likely to be useful as a fertile parent in a cross, but its existence is certainly interesting.

sieboldii 'Colossus' × *grandiflora* Breeder Dennis Ledvina of Greenbay, Wisconsin has repeated this cross numerous times with a variety of *M. grandiflora*

M. 'MARYLAND' X *GRANDIFLORA* at Magnolian Grove Arboretum

RICHARD FIGLAR

MAGNOLIA INSIGNIS MGA 355 X GRANDIFLORA 'KAY PARRIS' (*LEFT*) **COMPARED TO M. GRANDIFLORA 'KAY PARRIS'** (*RIGHT*) – is this hybrid the first step towards a pink *Magnolia grandiflora*?

RICHARD FIGLAR

IN CLOSING......

Several factors point toward a renewed interest in the species *Magnolia grandiflora*. Our lifestyles are continually becoming more urbanized, and future breeding work to develop columnar and compact cultivars will allow it to become an integral part of every garden, no matter how small.

Recent breakthroughs in interspecific hybridization have made the quest for a pink 'grandiflora' more than just a fleeting dream. Modern marketing efforts are placing a wide array of cultivars into the gardens of a greater cross section of society. One day there will be a 'flavor' that almost everyone can appreciate. But, we should not forget, or take for granted, the grandeur of some those 'Classics' and 'Oldies but Goodies' that best embody the epithet *Magnolia grandiflora*.

ACKNOWLEDGEMENTS

I would like to thank the following individuals and institutions for the information, images, insight and inspiration which they provided. Richard Figlar, Gary Knox and Emily Welch, Douglas Justice, John Allman, Jenks Farmer, Thierry Lamant, Greg Paige, Bob Head, Pat McCracken, Andrew Bunting, Milliken and Company, Wofford College, Spartanburg Community College and the Spartanburg Regional Healthcare System.

I would also like to dedicate this article to the memory of my brother-in-law Richard Robinson Jr, who left us way too soon on September 8th, 2011.

SOURCES

Brailsford Sr, JF. 'Magnolia grandiflora 'Claudia Wannamaker''. *Journal of the Magnolia Society.* (1988) Vol. 23(2). Issue 44. 1–4. Callaway, DJ. *The World of Magnolias.* Timber Press, Portland, Oregon (1994). Dirr, MA. *Manual of Woody Landscape Plants.* Stipes Publishing, Champaign, Illinois (Sixth Edition) (2009). Figlar, RB. 'New cultivars of *Magnolia grandiflora*'. *Journal of the Magnolia Society.* (1988) Vol. 23(2). Issue 44. 1–4. McDaniel, JC. 'There is variety in evergreen magnolias.' *Brooklyn Botanical Gardens Record* (1973) 29(3): 18–21. Parris, et al. 'Ploidy Levels, Relative Genome Sizes, and Base Pair Composition in Magnolia.' *Journal of the American Society for Horticultural Science.* (2010) 135: 533–547.

Kevin Parris

has an MS in Plant and Environmental Sciences from Clemson University and is Horticulture Instructor and Arboretum Director of Spartanburg Community College, South Carolina

Lasting care for camellias: pruning

JENNIFER TREHANE

UNWELCOME VISITORS? *CAMELLIA* 'ADOLPHE AUDUSSON' & *C. X WILLIAMSII* 'DONATION' make their presence felt in a big way!
JENNIFER TREHANE

YOU MAY HAVE a great fondness for 'Adolphe Audusson' but do you really want him stepping through the front door? 'Berenice Boddy' was undoubtedly a delightful lady as was 'Cecile Brunazzi' but should they be invading your bedrooms through the windows, large as life and blocking out the light? Should they be allowed to get away with it?

The *Camellia* x *williamsii* 'Donation' illustrated is slightly different: it has an excuse. This plant was photographed in Norway after the severe winter of 2009/2010 and, because it was planted so very close to a house, was the only happy, flowering camellia I saw the following May. Nonetheless, it really should be pruned.

DRASTIC MEASURES ARE THE ONLY ANSWER HERE
JENNIFER TREHANE

THIS *CAMELLIA* 'INSPIRATION' IS JUST TOO OVERPOWERING   JENNIFER TREHANE

HOW PLANTS MAY LOOK A FEW MONTHS AFTER PRUNING (*ABOVE*) AND A YEAR LATER (*BELOW*)
JENNIFER TREHANE

Camellias, like children, should not be allowed to dominate and, if already out of control, may need drastic treatment. Of course it's better to bring them up with a modicum of discipline in the first place.

The much loved camellias illustrated have got out of control and, hard though it may be, drastic measures are needed. In the case of the camellias outside the bungalow opposite it was a chain saw job; they were cut nearly to ground level the following February and duly sprouted from the remaining 20cm of trunk the following summer. Over the next couple of years, if this sort of action is taken, there is a possibility of a dense thicket forming, with the need to thin the young shoots in order to give space for the remaining ones to flower. Blooms can be expected two to three years after such drastic pruning.

Another alternative would have been to cut branches back with a pruning saw and seca-teurs, leaving one or two smaller green shoots here and there if possible, but otherwise ending up with what the New Zealanders call 'a hat rack' of bare branches. This gives an existing framework from which new branches will grow.

Either way, drastic pruning is hard to contemplate but it does produce a new, more manageable bush from the old.

PRUNED CAMELLIAS AND SUMMER BEDDING
JENNIFER TREHANE

A third option is the one most often used, especially if the main problem is height. Some camellia varieties can exceed five metres in height at maturity and become too dominant after ten to fifteen years. They may stop the traffic when in bloom but are really too much of a statement during the rest of the year.

The easiest thing to do is to chop the top portion of the bush/bushes back to a chosen height and then, if too broad, use the secateurs or hedge trimmers to cut growth back all round. This makes for very dense bushes over the years, great for nesting birds, an excellent background for summer bedding, but maybe not so good if it is a show of camellia blooms that is wanted.

A CALIFORNIAN EXHIBITOR'S 'YARD'
JENNIFER TREHANE

Skilled thinning of branches to space them out is possible; in fact some of the 'Show fraternity' in the USA, who go for really enormous blooms in their competitions, prune their bushes so drastically in order to give each flower plenty of space to expand, that their bushes hardly look like camellias at all. Not a pretty sight.

**BEAUTY BORNE OF CREATIVE PRUNING –
NO MORE NEED TO 'TIPTOE' AROUND THIS
CAMELLIA!**
JENNIFER TREHANE

There are other options:

Standards
I know one gardener whose gateway at the side of the house was being blocked by *C.* x *williamsii* 'Tiptoe', so he removed all the lower branches and created a 'standard', which at first looked a bit rough round the stem but gradually settled down to make an interesting and very showy plant.

'CLOUD PRUNING' TAKES CONTROL TO A TOTALLY DIFFERENT LEVEL   JENNIFER TREHANE

Topiary

In Japan the autumn-blooming sasanqua camellias, with their naturally fine growth and small leaves, are often shaped as topiary in the traditional 'cloud pruning' manner. Attractive even when not in bloom.

Espaliers

For camellias that naturally produce widely spaced, vigorous branches, there is the option to train plants as espaliers or fans against a wall or fence.

Bonsai

The ultimate solution!

ESPALIER TRAINING IS REALLY EFFECTIVE WITH SOME CAMELLIA VARIETIES   JENNIFER TREHANE

BONSAI PROVIDES THE ULTIMATE SOLUTION TO TAMING CAMELLIAS

WHEN TO PRUNE

Traditionally the advice has been to do the main pruning just before shoot growth starts in the spring. This means, for most varieties, immediately after blooming, if necessary cutting back branches that are still bearing blooms; these make attractive vases for the house.

In practice, pruning can be carried out at any time over the winter while plants are dormant and all the liquid sap is stored and immobilised as starch granules under the bark.

AND AFTERWARDS?

If the pruned bushes had trunks and branches of sufficient dimensions, keen woodworkers/woodturners might like to store them to season the wood for future use. Camellia wood is a useful hardwood for making small artefacts such as spinning tops, bowls and wooden dolls, I've even seen a coffee table made from camellia wood. Now that's an excellent conversation piece!

DISCIPLINE FROM THE BEGINNING

If space is limited and plants are grown in pots or tubs, or planted out in small gardens, where there is room for only a few favoured plants, more care needs to be taken in the choice of variety.

It is always better to choose those that are naturally compact and slow growing. They may not need pruning at all.

Those that have masses of blooms over a long flowering period probably give the best value, and need the least discipline. Some, such as C. 'Spring Festival', even have attractive bronze or reddish young growth too. However, many varieties send out quite long, strong, straight shoots in the later part of summer. If they are cut back to the main body of the bush in late winter this will help encourage branching behind the cut and keep the bush neat and compact.

A COLOURFUL RANGE OF CAMELLIA ARTEFACTS
JENNIFER TREHANE

Jennifer Trehane

is an internationally renowned camellia expert and current editor of the International Camellia Society Journal

The rhododendron legacy of the Magor family of Lamellen, Cornwall: an historical perspective

JOHN HAMMOND

LAMELLEN – LOOKING DOWN FROM THE FRONT TERRACE TOWARDS THE SHELTERED PONDS

PAM HAYWARD

STANDING ON THE FRONT TERRACE of Lamellen House in the early Spring and looking down the valley, with its banks clothed in a myriad of colours of bloom set against a host of shades of green, it is difficult to imagine that in 1900 this vista was open swathes of grassland with few clusters of trees. In the valley bottom, alongside the drive, the stream gathers momentum as it rushes downhill for three quarters of a mile to meet the River Allen, close by the Lodge and the entrance gates on the Wadebridge to Camelford road.

First appearances can be deceiving, as Lamellen is far older than the early-Victorian house would suggest. There is an entry for 'Lamdmanual' in the Domesday Book for at least one house on the site in 1086.[1] By 1280 this had evolved to 'Lamailwyn', meaning 'Valley of the Mills', and the 1698 date stone set in the western elevation of the present structure is from the earlier house built on the site by Samuel Furnis.

It is even more difficult to comprehend that Edward John Penberthy Magor, the quiet, reserved, unassuming English gentleman and founder of this peaceful garden, should become the mentor known as 'Mr Magor' to a brotherhood of early rhododendron pioneers in remote homesteads located in Massachusetts, New Jersey, Pennsylvania, Oregon, Vancouver Island, Australia, New Zealand and Germany. How was it that this rhododendron enthusiast came to the notice of other early rhododendron pioneers scattered across the globe? Why did he remain the focus of these pioneers for over 25 years before disappearing from the scene as quietly as he had arrived? Why, outside of his fellow rhododendron peers, have his endeavours remained unknown and are unrecognised in Britain?

Across the years, articles in several overseas publications have made reference to the support that the North American rhododendron pioneers received from a few gentlemen gardeners and institutions in Great Britain and Ireland in the years between 1918 and 1950. Key amongst the gentlemen gardeners was 'Mr Magor' of Lamellen; Lionel de Rothschild of Exbury and Charles P Raffill of RBG, Kew. Key amongst the institutions was the RBG, Edinburgh, RBG, Kew and Glasnevin Botanic Gardens, Dublin. Indeed, with the addition of John Guille Millais of Comptons Brow, JC Williams of Caerhays and Sir Edmund Loder of Leonardslee, the same individuals and institutions were the main supporters of the landed gentry in Great Britain and Ireland who were seeking plants or advice in regard to developing a woodland garden in the same timeframe. EJP Magor, who is usually referred to as 'Mr Magor' in old articles and documents, and for continuity we will do likewise, was in his own way a remarkable, if unrecognised, pioneer who was active in the field of rhododendrons until the onset of WWII.

His son, Major Walter M Magor, had entered the army to escape from the depressions of the 1930s and served in India, Iran and North Africa, including two periods with the Indian Political Service. The curtains close and open again in 1961 when Walter eventually returned to Lamellen, by which time the gardens had returned to nature. He was to face a monumental task of restoration to return them to their original glory, a task that ultimately was to be inherited by his daughter, Felicity, and her husband, Jeremy Peter-Hoblyn. This article aims to provide a wider perspective of the Magor dynasty, the network of rhododendron pioneers, and the forging of several special relationships that were not hindered by one's station in life, or hampered by the highly competitive arena between gentlemen gardeners that encompassed the introduction of new species and new hybrids in Britain and Ireland.

Given that it is around 70 years since the death of most of the key players in this story, it is unlikely that a definitive sequence of events that led to many of Mr. Magor's 'connections' will ever be known; however, there are now sufficient pieces of the jigsaw in-situ for a chronology to be outlined in detail. It is possible to be definitive, as a result of research work carried out at Lamellen and elsewhere, as to the sources of the rhododendrons that were raised in this plantsman's garden and the origins of the wild collected seed. Threads from other historical background notes have been woven in to the narrative as these provide a much clearer perspective of Mr. Magor's acquaintances, many of whom walk across the pages of this story and each in their own way were 'characters' in the Edwardian sense of the word, with influence in many spheres of life.

THE ORIGINS OF THE LAMELLEN ESTATE

The Magor family originated from Mousehole Parish in West Cornwall, and were brewers – Reuben Magor and William Davey having founded the Redruth Brewery in 1742, using pure water from an old mine. By this date the town was hemmed in on all sides by extensive mining works engaged in large-scale tin production, the extraction of copper and small amounts of lead and silver.[2] Over the years 1790 to 1802 the brewery was reformed under the name of Magor & Davey Co, and was gradually moved to a new location in 1792 where much of its plant was constructed in 1802. Reuben Magor and Edmund Turner were also partners in a bank at Kenwyn, Truro, under the title of

EDWARD J P MAGOR C.1910 contemporary with the time he was laying out the garden   LAMELLEN ESTATE RECORDS

the most extensive. Records indicate that the family had a long time interest in gardening, including orchids, and their connections with the Royal Cornwall Horticultural Society date back to at least 1838 when John P Magor exhibited material of *Salvia patens* at a meeting in Truro. Around 1835 James Veitch, who had recently relocated his nursery closer to Exeter, had the foresight to realise that the key to his company's prosperity lay in the improvement of tech-niques for seed germination and cultivation. He lured a promising young man named John Dominy (1816–1891) away from a rival nursery with the aim of building up his 'team'. [16, 18] Dominy turned out to be a wizard propagator and in 1842, just as the cases of William Lobb's seed collections in South America were spasmod-ically arriving at Topsham Dock at the head of the Exe estuary, he suddenly left James Veitch & Sons nursery in Exeter to work as Head Gardener for John P Magor. James Veitch's frustrations at losing his best nurseryman must have been immense – he spent the next four years trying to get Dominy back. He eventually succeeded in attracting Dominy to work at the Coombe Wood Branch in 1846, but this episode serves to illustrate the considerable influence John P Magor had in the gardening circles of Devon and Cornwall.

Messrs Turner & Magor, later Magor, Turner & Co. Penventon House, home of Reuben Magor's family, stood in its own grounds on the edge of the town, and in 1825 Elizabeth Ann Moyle, the only surviving child of Samuel Furnis's grandson John Furnis, and heiress of the Lamellen estate, married Reuben's son, John Penberthy Magor (1788–1862).[3]

Together they replaced the original Penventon House with a completely new Georgian mansion and the grounds were laid out as parkland and enhanced by additional planting of specimen trees. A second phase of expansion of the brewery commenced in 1834, and by 1841 the principle proprietor, John Penberthy Magor of Penventon, was one of the leading figures in the town, his business interests being one of

In the mid-1840s Elizabeth Magor inherited the Lamellen Estate from her father, John Furnis, the original house having been built by her grandfather, Samuel Furnis in 1698. Together, John and Elizabeth rebuilt the earlier house in the Picturesque Elizabethan Style and regularly stayed with their cousins, the Hext Family of Tremeer, to oversee the reconstruction. Work was completed in

LOOKING DOWN THE VALLEY IN C.1900 prior to the development of the garden by EJP Magor
LAMELLEN ESTATE RECORDS

1849.[13] Tremeer, 'just across the fields' from Lamellen, has benefited substantially in terms of plant material as a result of the continued relationship between the owners over the generations.

When John and Elizabeth came to live at Lamellen the valley was mainly pasture and parkland, with clusters of trees, which is reflected in a fading photograph from around 1900 that depicts wide swathes of open grassed areas around the House.[12] There are few records of when the basic tree planting was actually carried out. The 'Flat-leaved Oak' (*Quercus sessiliflora*), that continued to be coppiced until around 1920, was the main component of the clusters of woodland and, prior to 1850, there were hardwood plantings of the tulip tree (*Liriodendron tulipifera*), elm (*Ulmus campestris*), ash (*Fraxinus excelsior*), lime (*Tilia europaea*), London plane, Spanish chestnut (*Castanea sativa*), Red horse chestnut, evergreen oak (*Q. ilex*) and beech (*Fagus sylvatica*). One of the latter, which blew down in around 1965, had 300 annual rings when

counted. Plantings of softwoods, originally for windbreaks, consisted of Monterey Pine (*Pinus radiata*), Monterey Cypress (*Cupressus macrocarpa*), Douglas Fir (*Pseudotsuga menziesii*), Monkey Puzzle (*Araucaria araucana*), larch (*Larix decidua*), and several species of *Abies*, *Picea*, *Chamaecyparis*, *Thuja* and many Irish Yews.[13] John P Magor planted Lawson Cypress (*Cupressus lawsoniana*), Japanese Red Cedar (*Cryptomeria japonica*) and Hinoki Cypress (*Chamaecyparis obtusa*) in 1885.[12]

One of the first things that John and Elizabeth did on their arrival at Lamellen was to construct a new greenhouse for their large orchid collection, which continued to be a major interest amongst gentlemen gardeners in the Victorian era until the devastating winters of 1890/91, 1893/94 and 1894/5. These winters decimated the orchid collections in the massive greenhouses of the landed gentry, their heating systems being unable to cope with the severity of the persistent 'twelve week frosts'. After they had recovered from the shock of losing their orchid collections, many turned their attention to establishing a rhododendron collection instead.

In 1861 one of John and Elizabeth's daughters, Mary Ann, married John Thomas Henry Peter of Chyverton (1810–1873), but he died in 1873 and they had no children. John and Elizabeth's two eldest sons died prior to their father, who, on 5th July, 1862, himself suffered a heart attack and was found dead on a train when it arrived at St Kew Highway (the nearest station to Lamellen, on the London & South Western Railway line to Wadebridge and Padstow). Lamellen Estate then passed to his third son, Edward Auriol Magor. He married Mary Caroline Chilcott in 1873 but passed away in 1883 at the early age of 34, leaving three sons and two daughters. This led to the eldest son, Edward John Penberthy Magor, born 1874, spending much of his boyhood at Chyverton with his 'Aunt Mamie' prior to attending Harrow and Trinity College, Oxford.[13]

This historical background helps to explain just a few of the many complex family relationships that existed between the owners of the great houses and gardens of Cornwall; 'connections' that have endured down through the generations, despite changes of ownership.

THE DEVELOPMENT OF LAMELLEN GARDEN
Plantings of *Rhododendron* 'Russellianum' (*ponticum* x *arboreum*), also known as *R.* 'Cornish Early Red', are a distinctive feature of the older Cornish gardens. Those at Lamellen date from prior to 1900, and were probably planted by John P Magor in 1885 when he was planting trees.[4,12] Edward John Penberthy Magor (Mr Magor) started gardening at Lamellen in 1901, at which date his mother was still living in the house. He was inspired to cultivate rhododendrons by the sight of a plant of *R. grande* (then known as *argenteum*) in flower in the Temperate House, at the RBG, Kew in 1900.[14]

Mr Magor had dreams of inheriting Chyverton estate from his Aunt Mamie, whose husband, John TH Peter, had died in 1873. His hopes were dashed when his aunt decided to leave the estate to a distant member of the Peter Family, even though he was no relation of her

husband's. Sadly, shortly after the aunt died in 1915, Chyverton was sold on by the inheritor.[13] The Holman Family bought the estate and subsequently created the now famous garden to the east of the house.

In 1901 Mr Magor, at the age of 27, had a clean palette to work with at Lamellen; this is borne out by a couple of faded photographs taken around 1900 depicting wide swathes of open grass around the House with clusters of mature trees. So the garden was made on land that had probably been used for open grazing.[12] Standing in an elevated position near the top of a small valley, the House looks out across the wide expanse of the garden as the valley sweeps around and then narrows on its way down to the Lodge and entrance gates. The soil is heavy loam for the most part, in some parts very shallow, and overlies slaty shale, except in the centre of the valley where there is blue clay underneath.

From the very start he was planting rhododendrons, purchased from Richard Gill of Tremough, James Veitch of Coombe Wood in Chelsea, James. G Reuthe of Bromley in Kent, T Smith of Daisy Hill Nursery in Newry, V N Gauntlett & Co of Redruth (prior to the nursery moving to Chiddingfold, Surrey in 1906) , R Barclay Fox at Penjerrick, Jonathan Rashleigh at Menabilly, and even the dwarf Siberian species *R. camtschaticum*, *R. anthopogon* and *R. parvifolium* from Messrs Hegel & Kesselring of St Petersburg in 1903. Between 1901 and 1906 Mr Magor travelled widely, visiting RBG, Edinburgh, RBG, Kew several times and Glasnevin Botanic Garden. His ledgers record the rhododendrons given to him by these institutions as well as plants that came from Mr Acton at Kilmacurragh in Ireland and Mr Daubuz at Killiow near Truro. Below the 'Farm Road' are several *R.* 'Boddaertianum' that came from Reuthe in November, 1908.[12]

Mr Magor kept meticulous records of all plant and tree acquisitions, including the locations they were planted and the date of their first flowering. Interestingly, *R. crassum*, a Forrest introduction of 1906, first flowered in Britain at Lamellen in 1914. Very early on, he realised the advantage of growing rhododendrons from wild collected seed and accompanied Reginald Farrer on his 1909 expedition to Switzerland to collect alpines. Farrer's expeditions to the European Alps were usually of a month's duration and the party *'travelled hard and far'*, an approach that was to be his undoing in later years. Farrer invited Mr Magor to join him on his first expedition to China in 1914 but he had recently married Gilian, and so, somewhat reluctantly, he let William Purdom go in his place.[12]

In 1912 Mr Magor inherited the Lamellen Estate, by which time he had made major steps in laying out the garden. Contrary to the widely held present-day perspectives, inheriting an estate in the early 1900s was not a recipe for an easy life. The estate encompassed a number of farms, houses, buildings, workers and tenants that generated a plethora of matters that needed to be attended to, in addition to his banking interests. Mr Magor was a very private individual in the time-honoured

EDWARD J P & GILIAN MAGOR at the front of Lamellen House, probably in the mid-1930s
LAMELLEN ESTATE RECORDS

traditions of the Victoria and Edwardian eras, a world that most present day enthusiasts have great difficulty in grasping. In the course of Mr Magor's work in the Family's banking business he would have compartmentalised the transactions with each of his many 'customers' to maintain the levels of privacy and etiquette that were expected, and this approach spilled over in to his personal life. He also segregated his business interests from his home life, so that his gardening interests were, to all intents and purposes, taken forward in another world with a completely different 'set' of friends, even if it happened to involve some individuals that had accounts at the bank.

Gardening friendships in Victorian and Edwardian times tended to be formally maintained via correspondence, even if a friend happened to live relatively close by, and in this, Mr Magor was no exception. It is often forgotten that the Royal Mail provided a real public service prior to WWII, with multiple deliveries to, and collections from, businesses in the local towns each weekday. So it would not be unusual for a letter posted early in the morning on the way to the bank to be delivered in a local town the same morning and for a reply to be placed in the mail the same day. In this way there was an ongoing exchange of letters between John Charles Williams at Caerhays Castle, George Johnstone of Trewithen and Mr Magor. However, even the correspondence between individual friends was compartmentalised to avoid any inadvertent chance of causing offence by divulging personal information to a third party. The more detailed discussions took place through the social medium of a formal invitation to dinner, which provided an opportunity for a walk around the garden, an inspection of the greenhouses and propagation work, and for the exchange of plant material and seed.

In the late 1800s and early 1900s the status of a particular individual within the closed ranks of the landed gentry was not only judged on the size of the estate and the house[s] they owned, but also took account of the gardens and woodlands, together with the rarity of the plants and trees they contained. So, there was considerable competition to obtain desirable plant material and trees, including newly introduced species and new hybrids from both home and overseas. Even the rare plant material that happened to fall in to the hands of the key nurserymen of the day tended to find its way to favoured 'customers' amongst the landed gentry. The landed gentry expected to be waited on by lesser mortals; thus anyone who provided a service, be it at an individual or business level, was deemed to be 'in trade' and thus part of a lower class. So, those in trade or business, for example, owning or running a nursery, would not be countenanced in terms of being permitted to participate in the social life of the upper classes. But that said, the nurserymen kept themselves to themselves, in very much the same way as the landed gentry did. When the formation of a *Rhododendron Society* was mooted at Lanarth, Cornwall in March 1915, then founded at the Chelsea Show of May 1916, its original members were all gentlemen of means, and by invitation only. Amongst the 16 Founder Members, none of whom were nurserymen, was Mr Magor.

MR MAGOR'S WILD COLLECTED SEED ACQUISITIONS

In 1899 Ernest Henry Wilson was chosen by Sir William Thiselton-Dyer, Director of RBG, Kew, to collect plants for James Veitch & Sons at Coombe Wood, Kingston on Thames. Charles P Raffill, Assistant Curator at RGB, Kew, explained the background in a letter to Del and Rae James of Eugene, Oregon, dated 13th December, 1948:[7]

'The British firm of James Veitch and Sons, nurserymen of Chelsea, London, sent out to China my old and esteemed friend, E. Henry Wilson as a collector. We had both been employed at Birmingham Botanic Gardens and afterwards came to Kew as students. He was here at the Botanic Gardens, Kew in 1897 and I came in 1898. We both studied Botany together but he was a year in advance of me ... We both passed advanced Botany courses and both of us intended to be Botanists but Wilson's funds ran short and he could not continue his studies, so he took a post with the great British nursery firm, James Veitch.'

When James Veitch began selling the rhododendrons raised from Wilson's 1899–1902 collections made in China, a handwritten listing of the plants that were available, dated 20th September 1907, was sent to Mr Magor.[12] Interestingly, Veitch's listing refers to the seed collection number and flower colour; no species names were used. From that year onwards Mr Magor received a listing, quoting the species (where known) and the collector's number of each plant that would be available that particular season. He reserved a selection of plants each year that Veitch had new introductions available; these are itemised in his ledgers and were delivered to Lamellen in October or November of that year.[12] Some of these are still heathy plants today, notably W.1523, the pink form of *R. calophytum*. Wilson continued to collect exclusively for Veitch on the 1903–1905 expedition and in total, Veitch raised 31 species of rhododendrons that were distributed under 49 seed numbers.

Wilson arrived back home in England in March 1905 and went immediately to Coombe Wood nursery to work on his collections. Ironically, his very success was to lead to the termination of his contract. Not only were his plant collecting expeditions deemed to be a great success, his success in raising the Chinese introductions, in collaboration with George Harrow at Coombe Wood, was to cause James Herbert concerns that Veitch's stock would flood the market. So it was that Herbert wrote to Kew on October 2nd, 1906:[18]

'After five years most satisfactory service Wilson's engagement is terminated with my firm . ... Very shortly there will be no work for him here . ... and I am taking the liberty of troubling you in the hope that during the next few months some suitable position may be open.'

Kew found him temporary work, but he soon took a botanical assistant's post, cataloguing collections from Asia for the Imperial Institute of Science in London. Meanwhile, he steadfastly swept aside all the advances of Professor Sargent of the Arnold Arboretum, Boston who was extremely keen to engage someone to collect in China on behalf of the Arnold Arboretum and an American syndicate of wealthy individuals. Sargent doggedly countered Wilson's refusals and, after protracted negotiations, he secured Wilson's agreement in September 1906 to make two further plant-collecting expeditions in 1907–1908 and 1910–1911.[22] Three English subscribers contributed to the 1907–1908

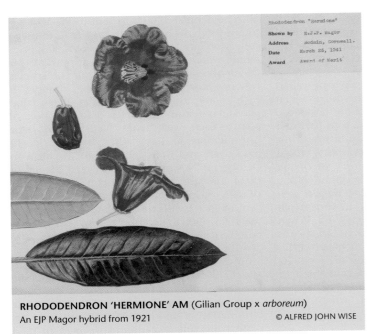

Rhododendron "Hermione"

Shown by   E.J.P. Magor
Address   Bodmin, Cornwall.
Date   March 28, 1941
Award   Award of Merit

RHODODENDRON 'HERMIONE' AM (Gilian Group x *arboreum*)
An EJP Magor hybrid from 1921   © ALFRED JOHN WISE

Far East and destined for delivery in England, normally entered the country through the port of Falmouth, as this was the most westerly safe harbour for the sailing ships to use. Mail, and other such traffic, was then shipped overland by road or rail. In due course the seed from Forrest's 1910–11 expedition arrived at Werrington Park, another estate owned by the Williams Family, at Launceston, on the border of Devon and Cornwall, and here JC Williams personally made up the packets of rhododendron seed and then distributed them to syndicate members and his friends. JC Williams also supervised the germination and plant cultivation at Werrington Park and initially the seedlings were planted out there rather than at his story-book castle at Caerhays. Mr Magor received seed of most of the species from this expedition and subsequently from the 1912–15, 1921–23 and 1924–26 expeditions.[12]

JC Williams was to sow seed of a different kind when, in 1915, he sent Mr Magor a copy of the newly published first edition of Bean's *Trees and Shrubs Hardy in the British Isles* with Walter Magor's name written on the fly-leaf, saying 'I hope the boy will make a gardener one day.'[13] Walter was then four years old.

With the arrival of Wilson's and Forrest's seed from China, Mr Magor ceased purchasing plants and concentrated on raising plants from seed. He regularly teased his wife about not going plant-hunting with Farrer in 1914; however, Sir George Holford sent him seed from the expedition and these were sown in early-1915.[12] Sir George Holford was a frequent visitor to Caerhays and JC Williams remarked that he was very discerning and difficult to please in terms of plant material.

expedition, including JC Williams of Caerhays Castle, Cornwall who, between 1909 and 1911, distributed seed of 28 species under 35 seed numbers from Wilson's latter expeditions. Williams sent seed to Mr Magor. As was the case with later plant collectors, it is highly likely that Wilson would have been invited to dine or stay with the owners of major Cornish gardens who had purchased selections of plants raised from his seed by Veitch, or shared the distribution of his later seed collections. In this way Magor would have met Wilson and had the opportunity to discuss matters relating to the collection of seed and the methodology of raising plants. Inexplicably, these two men from entirely different backgrounds would, in the passage of time, become the key facilitators in this story.

Lamellen garden benefited enormously from Mr Magor's friendship with JC Williams, then Lord Lieutenant of Cornwall who, jointly with the RBG, Edinburgh, sponsored George Forrest's 1910–11 expedition to China. Mail and time-conscious traffic such as seed and plant material, carried by packet boat from the

By the time Mr Magor was sowing Farrer's seed, Great Britain was well entrenched in the First World War. Many well-known gardens were severely affected by the loss of all their younger garden staff to fight in the trenches, and Cornwall was no exception. By the time hostilities had come to an end many large gardens had become overgrown and, with the continuing shortage of gardeners in the post-war economy, some estates never recovered, a noteworthy example being Heligan. It would be 1927 before Mr Magor obtained the services of a proficient replacement gardener.[13]

Another friend, Captain WH Schroeder, who started to grow rhododendron species at Attadale, near Inverewe, Ross-shire in 1920, sent him seed from Rock's 1923–24 and 1925–26 expeditions.[12] The volumes of seed that Rock collected were immense and often contained consecutive numbers of the same species which tended to cause difficulties for the gardeners who were faced with raising the large number of seed lots.

In keeping with his banking background Mr Magor meticulously recorded in his ledger, under the title of *Chinese Rhododendrons*, the date he received each seed-lot, the collector's number, the name of the species (where known), the dates the seed was sown, germinated, potted on, the location and date that the seedlings were planted out in the garden, the date and colour of the first flowering and names of other recipients of the seedlings he had raised.[12]

With the large quantities of seed coming to hand, together with the need for assessment of the huge quantities of seedlings being raised of species material that had not been seen previously by the recipients, it was little wonder that the learning curve was immense. Names of many of the species were subsequently amended by Mr Magor in the ledgers over the years in the light of detailed correspondence that dates from 1916 with JC Williams and Professor Bayley Balfour (later Sir Isaac), Regius Keeper at RBG, Edinburgh who made the first attempts to classify these new collections from China. Following Balfour's death in 1922 the correspondence continued unabated with HF Tagg and Sir William Wright Smith at Edinburgh, both being instrumental in taking the identification and classification work forward. These correspondents were well aware of the possibility of hybrids occurring in the wild in areas where two species met, and of the resulting taxonomic difficulties or confusion. They were also concerned with the variation in a species caused by a wide geographical distribution with differing climatic conditions. That their doubts were justified, especially in the case of rhododendrons raised from Wilson and Forrest's seed, is well demonstrated by the revisions of many series in the genus in later years, as the following example clearly indicates.

By 1914 Sir Harry Veitch was 74 years old and, as there was no one to 'inherit' the Veitch dynasty, it was decided to wind up the Coombe Wood business. A huge clearance sale of nursery stock, which commenced on November 10th 1914, resulted in many large lots being disposed of, ironically including most of Wilson's introductions. The auction at Coombe Wood ran on for ten days.[18] Prior to the sale Sir Harry Veitch invited a number of old friends and customers to have first choice of the specimen plants. Amongst other items, Mr Magor purchased a plant of Wilson's under W1539. Seven years later, in 1922, he sent a flower to Sir Isaac Bayley Balfour for identification. Balfour, having shown it to Wilson, who happened to be in the Herbarium at the time, determined that it had not yet been described and named it *R. magorianum*, a hardy member of the Irrorata subsection.[14] Unfortunately, some years later it was reassessed as a possible wild hybrid.

Two huge and very old magnolias, *Magnolia campbellii* and *M. delavayi*, which stand close to the east side of the House, are almost certainly from Wilson seed, and are thought to have been purchased from Coombe Wood, possibly at the time of Veitch's 1914 sale. Given the collections of magnolias that graced the gardens of many of Mr Magor's local acquaintances, it is somewhat intriguing that he never acquired a collection himself. Perhaps the answer can be found in the winter of early-1917, one of the most severe prior to 1940, which killed outright a number of tender rhododendrons at Lamellen and would have decimated many early-flowering magnolias throughout Cornwall.

MR MAGOR'S HYBRIDISATION PROGRAMME

Hybridisation was a subject that fascinated many early gentlemen gardeners in Cornwall with an interest in rhododendrons, and Mr Magor was no exception. He commenced his hybridisation programme with cross #1 in 1905 and, having corresponded with Professor Bayley Balfour about the correct way of approach, he made primary crosses with the species. Most of his hybrids bore 'portmanteau' names made from the first part of the two parent species names, with the seed parent placed first, as recommended by Balfour.[12]

Few rhododendron enthusiasts realise just how much hybridisation work Mr Magor accomplished – by the time of his death his listing of crosses had reached #2044, probably a record for a British plantsman with no commercial interests. In comparison, Lionel de Rothschild made 1210 crosses in a 22 year period, so the average number of crosses per year was very similar. As a precursor of the approach used in more recent years, he planted the hybrids out on trial in the garden in groups of three with a view to keeping the best. A total of 100 crosses were named of which 80 were registered in Mr Magor's lifetime, over 20 others have been registered since and there are many others that should have been named.

At the turn of the century, like many of his peers in rhododendron circles, Mr Magor used in his hybridisation programme each Spring the flowerings of whatever newly introduced species came into bloom for the first time. Competition to be the first to create a stunning hybrid from each new species was intense and, inevitably, in relatively few years the process resulted in the production of a range of 'look-alike' hybrids. The first to raise a good looking plant with an attractive truss usually got to name the cross, and it was the accepted practice for the plants raised from the same cross in other gardens to assume the same name, unless the characteristics of the flowers were markedly different. Probably the best known of Mr Magor's hybrids are R. 'Damaris', R. 'Lamellen', R. 'Cinnkeys', R. 'Gilian', R. 'Saint Breward' and R. 'Saint Tudy'.

Lionel de Rothschild closely monitored Mr Magor's approach to hybridisation and a took a good many batches of his seedlings back home to Exbury. Whilst walking around Exbury on 21st March 1938, Mr Lionel noted, *'A fine scarlet hybrid of MAGOR'S – 'Daphne' – with its curious double calyx is a pretty dwarf bush and makes a fine splash of colour against the dark fir trees.'* And, again on 5th April 1938, *'Haematodes x blood-red arboreum of MAGOR was fully out with fine trusses of amazing scarlet. The plants I have are quite first class and are a great credit to the raiser.'* [15] This latter cross would appear to be unnamed whereas R. 'Daphne', a 1921 cross of R. 'Red Admiral' x R. neriiflorum, was named after Mr Magor's daughter-in-law and received an AM in 1933. Many of Mr Magor's crosses have been used by later generations of enthusiasts in their hybridisation programmes, including Dietrich Hobbie in Germany.

THE SPRING MEETING OF THE *RHODODENDRON SOCIETY*

As late as 1925 membership of the exclusive *Rhododendron Society* numbered only 23 in total. Ernest H Wilson, who had been elected as an honorary member, commented that it was illiberal for the information being distributed to members to be classified as confidential. Lionel de Rothschild was a key instigator of discussions in 1925 as to the practicability of opening up the society to other gardeners who were requesting membership. In 1927 a new organisation under the title of the *Rhododendron Association* was formed [incorporated 1928] and was open to all who wished to join, subject to election. However, the original *Rhododendron Society* continued in being as a private organisation with a fixed membership, and from 1927 until the 1939 outbreak of hostilities, the key members of the *Rhododendron Society* gathered each Spring at Lamellen, the usual attendees being: [12] Lionel N de Rothschild of Exbury, Hampshire, Henry McLaren of Bodnant, North Wales [later the 2nd Lord Aberconway], Colonel Stephenson R Clark of Borde Hill, Sussex, JB Stevenson of Tower Court, Surrey [attendee

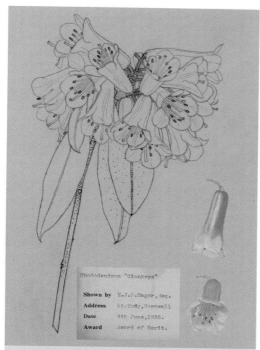

RHODODENDRON 'CINNKEYS' AM
A famous Magor hybrid of *cinnabarinum* x *keysii*
raised in 1917   © ALFRED JOHN WISE

Meath, Ireland had been laid out by him in the same time-frame as Lamellen. Lord Headfort sent Mr Magor seed from Kingdon Ward's 1921, 1922 and 1924–25 expeditions.[12]

DISTRIBUTION OF MR MAGOR'S PLANTS IN BRITAIN

The commentary on Mr Magor's wild collected seed acquisitions, hybridisation programme and the listing of regular visitors to Lamellen serves to emphasise that he was uniquely well placed to provide both plant material and knowledge from detailed 'hands-on' experience that dated from the time when 'Chinese Rhododendrons' first arrived in Britain. Mr Magor's ability to source material and act as a facilitator was greatly enhanced by fact that his immediate friends in the world of rhododendrons were the key figures of the era, so he was able to source plant material from collections in other major British and Irish gardens.

One of the most significant, and perhaps least known of Mr Magor's activities was his involvement in distributing both species and hybrids to 'gentleman gardeners' by the circulation of a 'List of Surplus Plants for Sale'.[13] This list was being distributed as early as 1918 and by the 1920s there was a 'network' in place whereby the landed gentry were able to sell or exchange surplus plants and thereby service each other's needs; however, it was not realised until recently just how large a volume was involved. Around 1915 John A Holms, who was landscaping and developing gardens around the new mansion house on his Formakin Estate near Bishopton, Renfrewshire, became infected with an extremely bad case of *rhododendronitis*. Holms had already developed an insatiable appetite as a serious collector in the fields of antique furniture, works of art, tapestries and porcelain, so it was second nature to him to direct his organisational skills to acquiring rhododendrons. Holms was also a perfectionist and he meticulously recorded all his plant acquisitions for the development of the gardens around his new country house, and then later, in connection with the development of the

from 1929], H Armytage Moore of Rowallane, Northern Ireland [attendee from 1929], Sir Frederick Moore [retired from Glasnevin, Dublin in March, 1922 and usually accompanied H Armytage Moore], Lord Headfort of Headfort, Southern Ireland [attendee from 1929], Lord Stair of Castle Kennedy, South West Scotland [attendee from 1929] and EJP Magor of Lamellen, Cornwall.

Many of these attendees were given, exchanged or purchased large selections of rhododendrons whilst visiting Lamellen and other gardens in the area, and in this way plants from Cornwall, both species and hybrids, spread all over the Great Britain and Ireland. Typical of the attendees, whose name may not be familiar, was Mr Magor's friend Lord Headfort (1878–1943), whose garden and arboretum at Headfort House, Kells, Co

major rhododendron garden he developed at an unlikely, undulating, rocky, woodland location called Larachmhor, at Arisaig on Scotland's West Coast. Holms classified Mr Magor as a 'Rhododendron Dealer', one of fifteen names in a listing that included all the 'key' nurseries of the day, which at first sight seems inappropriate. In the period April 1918 to October 1919 four batches of plants were ordered from Mr Magor and delivered to Formakin Estate, comprising in total 15 species and 4 hybrids. In contrast, between November 26th 1926 and November 1930 ten batches of plants were supplied for Larachmhor Garden comprising 102 species, 90 small species seedlings, 64 hybrids (including some of Mr Magor's best crosses) and 32 small hybrid seedlings.[20] Many were large plants around 5 to 6ft high, costing up to £3 per plant; some were rare specimens costing up to £10 per plant; the minimum charge per plant was 5 shillings. Interestingly, Mr Magor's named hybrids were significantly more expensive than the species. These statistics provide but a glimpse of the scope of Mr Magor's propagation work, since Holms was just one of his many contacts who were seeking plants. What is of far more significance is the wide range of both species and hybrid material that Mr Magor had on offer in his listings each year. We can but wonder where he found the time to propagate single-handedly, or the nursery space to raise such a large inventory of plants at Lamellen. Will Haughton, the gardener, came to Lamellen in 1927, after service as a cook in the Navy, and lived at the Lodge with his wife. Mr Magor gave him explicit instructions never to touch any of the rhododendrons in the nurseries or the gardens, which he faithfully adhered to.[13]

Edward 'Walter' Moyle Magor, Mr Magor's son, had the unusual distinction of taking a degree in Botany at both Oxford and Cambridge, his thesis being *The Flora and Fauna of Bodmin Moor*, which remains an invaluable source of reference. Frustrated by his inability to find employment where he could use his knowledge of botany, he decided to escape the 1930s depression and follow his equestrian interests instead by taking a commission with the Indian Army – Poona Horse. Later he resigned from the services, married Daphne Davis Graham in 1939, and then succeeded in finding employment in the Indian Political Service.[10]

MR MAGOR AND THE NORTH AMERICAN RHODODENDRON PIONEERS

A long, detailed article published in 2004 – *Mr Magor and the North American Triangle: An Historical Perspective*[16] – provides an insight into the highly significant part that Mr Magor played in supporting the establishment of three geographically disparate rhododendron pioneers, and the following is a brief outline. Ernest Wilson was to play the role of an un-remarked facilitator in this story, and thus brought together the four key players.

George Fraser *(ABOVE LEFT)* emigrated in 1881 from Perthshire, Scotland to Canada and in 1886 eventually arrived in Victoria on Vancouver Island in search of land suitable for raising rhododendrons and heathers. He purchased 256 acres of native bush in 1892 for $256 at the isolated frontier location of Ucluelet. He put up a shack and cleared nine acres of land to start a nursery, but even with a horticultural background as a head gardener, he had a hard struggle setting up in business as a nurseryman. In 1906 Fraser, who was seeking sources of rhododendron plant material, made contact with Ernest H Wilson, who was back at the RBG, Kew in a temporary capacity, but he was unable to help at that time. In April 1919 Professor Sargent arranged the appointment of Wilson as Assistant Director of the Arnold Arboretum and around this date George Fraser corresponded with Wilson at the Arnold Arboretum seeking to obtain seed.[8] This time Wilson could help and provided Fraser with a listing of names to contact in England as he would have been aware of JC Williams's distribution network based in Cornwall. Fraser struggled to get a positive response to his letters, but in the passage of time received a reply from a Mr Magor of Lamellen. So the first transatlantic 'connection' fell in to place and records suggest that seed was sent to Fraser in Ucluelet, BC each year from around 1922.[12, 21]

In late 1919 Joseph B Gable *(OPPOSITE BELOW LEFT)*, a nurseryman of Stewartstown, Pennsylvania also made contact with Wilson at the Arnold Arboretum. Gable appears to have been searching for plant material and other nurserymen with an interest in rhododendrons, so Wilson put Gable in touch with Fraser, and so began a lifelong exchange of correspondence.[9] The continuing correspondence between Fraser and Gable served to underline the problems that Gable faced in raising seedlings that could survive the extremes of the East Coast climate. In the mid-1920s Fraser decided to 'introduce' Gable to Mr Magor by mail so the two could directly discuss the performance of seedlings raised in Pennsylvania from Lamellen seed.[8]

James Elwood Barto *(RIGHT)*, born in Philadelphia, Pa on June 14th 1881, was a US Naval shipyard specialist-carpenter by trade, having first enlisted in 1905. After the WWI armistice was signed, Barto travelled west to Oregon in 1920, having heard that certain lands were available to veterans for homesteading. Barto filed a claim for around 160 acres of land densely covered with Douglas fir and interspersed with oak, maple, alder, wild cherry and red cedar on the High Pass Road, ten miles west of Junction City. He returned home to Chicago, loaded his wife, kids and whatever else they could fit into an old chain-driven truck and headed back west to Oregon. As the family would later recall, this was a 2,700 mile nightmare of a journey and several weeks were to elapse before they arrived in Eugene in October, 1920. Barto found work in Eugene as a carpenter and at weekends he worked long hours at the High Pass Road property clearing timber and a heavy understorey of vine maple and other shrubs on a small area of land where he completed the erection of a temporary log cabin in June, 1921.[17]

Barto developed an interest in rhododendrons and azaleas whilst doing carpentry work at Raup & York's nursery in Eugene and learnt much of his cultivation methodology from the work of Raup, who provided him with seed to experiment with at the homestead. The seed germinated well in a tray placed on top of Mrs Barto's chicken incubator that was heated by a kerosene lamp. Barto was 'hooked' on rhododendrons. Around 1926 he contacted Mrs ACU Berry, a plantswoman of wide-ranging interests, who was constructing a large garden in an uptown area of Portland, Oregon. Mrs Berry was well-connected in horticultural circles, was also a subscriber to a number of major plant collecting expeditions and she gave Barto a list of names to contact.[11] This list included the contact details for Ernest H Wilson who in turn provided Barto with the contact details for George Fraser on Vancouver Island.[17] Barto wrote to Fraser, who in turn exchanged some thoughts in correspondence with Gable about the 'new kid on the block', prior to responding to Barto. In due course both Fraser and Gable came to realise that they both had difficulty in servicing the deluge of correspondence, queries and requests for specific plant material that Barto generated, so Fraser wrote to Mr Magor in early 1927 to 'introduce' Barto by mail.[8] This put in place the 'triangle' that became the North American end of the 'connection' that corresponded with Mr Magor. Records indicate that he sent seed to the USA every year from 1927 until 1940, mainly in response to requests for specific species seed, and he often enclosed additional material, including seed from his own hybridisation work.[9, 11] After 1930 pollen was also regularly sent in response to many requests and in some years, scions and seedlings were also forwarded.[17]

Reference has been made earlier to Edinburgh RBG's concerns arising from the doubtful status of herbarium specimens of, and seedlings propagated from, many of the early collectors numbers. Past articles and surviving correspondence suggest that both Gable and Barto were dedicated 'collectors' of rhododendron species rather than just traditional gardeners. Their correspondence indicates they exchanged seed of specific collector's numbers and sought to extend their own species collections whenever the opportunity arose. Records also suggest that they requested specific collector's numbers in their letters to Mr. Magor and other correspondents in Great Britain. Not surprisingly, the Gable correspondence contains a number of comments referring to the difficulties of identifying which seedlings were true to type and which were hybrids, which replicated the problems that faced British pioneers who were raising wild collected seed.[21]

THE DIFFICULT THIRTIES AND FORTIES SIGNAL THE END OF AN ERA

Ernest H Wilson and his wife Nellie were returning to their South Street, Boston home from a visit to their daughter in Geneva, NY State on October 15th, 1930 when their car spun off the road and dropped 40 feet down an embankment near Worcester, Mass. Nellie was dead when she was pulled from the wreck and Wilson died of his injuries an hour later.[22] Tragically, this highway accident brought to an end the key role of facilitator that Wilson had played in this story since the turn of the century.

In the mid-1930s Eric Savill, Deputy Ranger of Windsor Great Park, began laying-out what are now the Savill and Valley Gardens and, as the work progressed, he began to seek donations of rhododendron plants for the gardens. Mr Magor was very pleased to let Eric have a good many of the foundation plants. Soon after the introduction of petrol rationing in 1940, Eric Savill, accompanied by Lord Strathcona, brought a 3-ton truck to Cornwall and filled it with rhododendrons from Caerhays Castle, Lamellen and Trewithen.[13]

In 1937 Koichiro Wada sent seed of *R. metternichii* var. *metternianum* from the Izu Peninsula in Japan, and in return plants were sent by Mr Magor. Dietrich Hobbie visited Lamellen shortly after Wada's seed arrived and he obtained a portion of that seed. Hobbie's tour of gardens in Cornwall made a lasting impression on him, and Mr Magor sent plants to him, which provided a great impetus to his work.[13] Boxes of un-flowered seedlings, both species and hybrids, were sent by Mr Magor to gardens throughout the British Isles for at least two decades prior to WWII.

James Elwood Barto became very ill in early 1940 and sought admission to the Veterans Administration Hospital in Portland, Oregon where he was admitted for medical care in May, 1940. Sadly, he was found to have cancer and in June of the same year his home burned to the ground and with it his library and all his records. He passed away at the hospital on December 22nd, 1940.[17, 19]

With Britain deeply embedded in WWII, Edward John Pemberthy Magor was never to meet the pioneers he had stoically supported, as he passed away quietly on 14th May 1941.[13] It was the end of an era; by the time the WWII hostilities had come to an end most of the overseas rhododendron personalities, who had maintained contact with Mr Magor, had also passed away. For two decades Mr Magor had been the catalyst by which large volumes of rhododendron seed, pollen, scions and plants, both species and hybrids, together with detailed advice on propagation and cultivation, had found their way to the North American pioneers. Though Mr Magor, in his lifetime, was never to realise the significance of his legacy, this unlikely pioneer was to influence and strike the imagination of later generations of rhododendron enthusiasts and gardeners on both the East Coast of the USA and across the Pacific Northwest.

The eloquent words of Joseph Gable in a letter dated January, 8th 1942 to Guy Nearing, another early rhododendron pioneer from Ridgewood, New Jersey, expresses the debt owed to Mr Magor by a good many early rhododendron enthusiasts:[21]

'Well our good old friend Mr Magor has passed on and I am sure if rhododendron lovers had any share in building up his future reward in the life to come he would not want. Letters from Australia, New Zealand, Chile, Japan and Germany that I can recall, all praised him for his disinterested generosity in helping them to obtain their wants. That he appreciated a little of this in return I well know for he once wrote me that out of the hundreds of recipients of seed, etc. from him I was one of the few who not only thanked him but reciprocated in kind. Nothing was too much trouble for him it seemed. If he did not have the seed I wanted himself he would go fifty miles to a neighbor's garden or send to Edinburgh Botanic or to Ireland before he would abandon the effort – and then apologize – a true old English gentleman.

And I just had a Christmas note from Mr Fraser of Ucluelet, Vancouver Island, who first introduced me – by mail – to Mr Magor. So to these two men more than all the others – I owe my acquisitions in the first few years of my rhododendron growing.'

In his memory, the Cornwall Garden Society introduced the 'EJP Magor Memorial Cup' for rhododendrons. More recently, the American Rhododendron Society posthumously presented their most prestigious, and rarely given honour, the 'Pioneer Achievement Award,' to EJP Magor at their National Convention held in Vancouver, WA in May 2011. The citation notes that '...Mr Magor must have done more towards the start of Rhododendron growing in the USA and Canada than any other person in Britain.'[23]

LAMELLEN RETURNS TO NATURE AND THE UPHILL STRUGGLE TO RESTORE THE GARDEN

At the outbreak of WWII Walter M Magor had re-joined the newly mechanised Poona Horse and was sent to North Africa, where he was dispatched on dangerous reconnaissance missions to ensure that the important route to India via Iran remained open.[10] He returned briefly to Lamellen when his father passed away and his mother, Gilian, did not feel able

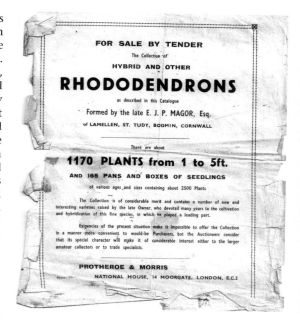

to live on at Lamellen by herself, so the house was let for many years.

1,170 seedlings and young plants, 1–5ft (0.3–1.5m) in cold frames were listed in a large catalogue produced by Protheroe & Morris of London and sold off by tender with a return date of 31st July 1941. Many passed into good hands, including Lord Aberconway, Mr Balfour, RHS Wisley, John B Stevenson, Colonel Clark, Lord Strathcona and MP Williams. Will Haughton, the gardener, stayed on at the Lodge with his wife after Mr Magor's death, and did not finally retire until 1969. Mr Magor had never let him touch the rhododendrons, so he faithfully adhered to his instructions, and just kept the lawns, kitchen garden and drive tidy, scythed the brambles and bracken each autumn around the rhododendrons and, with Britain in the midst of WWII, the rest of the garden quietly went to sleep.[13]

George Fraser enjoyed his life in the small isolated community of Ucluelet and passed away on 3rd May 1944 after 50 years of raising rhododendrons and playing his fiddle at the community dances. And, like Barto before him, Fraser's correspondence that he had

DAPHNE M MAGOR, probably in the mid-1940s
LAMELLEN ESTATE RECORDS

of courage and vision for an amateur gardener to embark upon what was by any standards a major restoration project. Immediately prior to the onset of WWII he obtained a considerable number of plants from Mr Magor, and a further selection was obtained from Lamellen in the 1950s when Tremeer garden was being restored. In the passage of time this action would prove to be fortuitous, as otherwise some original plants would have been lost.[5]

Following the cessation of hostilities in 1945, Major Walter M Magor remained overseas in the Political Service in India, dispensing justice in strife-ridden Northern India until the 1947 partition. He then joined the Kenyan Colonial Administration and was in Nairobi during the Mau Mau uprising. Walter stayed on in Nairobi and helped the Belgians to flee from the Congo, and in 1961 received the Medaille de la Belgique Reconnaisante for this act. But 1961 was to be an important year in other ways as Walter returned with Daphne to England to take up a post at the Board of Trade in London, providing him with the opportunity to realise his dream of living permanently at his Lamellen birthplace.[10]

None of the multiple tenants of Lamellen House had been interested in looking after garden in the years following the death of Mr Magor; indeed, there had not been a tenant in the House for four years prior to 1961. Walter arrived at the Lodge to find the driveway completely blocked by a large branch of a tall cherry tree, and this had to be removed to allow the furniture van to get up the drive, which badly needed resurfacing. But this was only the start, as the severe cutting back of conifers, laurels and rhododendrons continued, as in some places they met in the middle of the three-quarters of a mile long drive. Daphne was faced with sorting out an indescribable mess left by tenants in the House, whilst Walter commuted to London to spend weekdays at the Board of Trade. It was to be 1962 before any serious attention was paid to reclamation of the garden, and this was to be a year of discovery, spent largely identifying what had actually survived. Fortunately, welcome assistance in

carefully kept over the years was all destroyed after his death in a fire at his home.[8] Mr Magor's ledgers and scrapbooks contain extensive plant records, articles and newspaper cuttings relating to plants and cultivation techniques, but very little in the way of correspondence. His family have suggested that to maintain confidentiality he may have destroyed correspondence that did not contain information of specific long-term interest.

Colonel Eric GWW Harrison, later Major-General, had bought Tremeer in 1939, at which time the garden was derelict, but the intervention of WWII delayed its restoration and work did not begin to save the garden from ruin until 1947. It required a great deal this task came from the RBG, Edinburgh. Walter and Daphne also decided to start showing again, both in Cornwall and in London, and the judges provided a great deal of encouragement.[6, 13]

Daphne invested a considerable amount of her time and energy during 1963 and 1964 single-handedly reclaiming the jungle that had grown up over the past 20 years, including cutting back the bamboo (*A. palmata*) that was rampant throughout the half-acre basin in front of the house, and mowing the grass. Walter spent what time he had at weekends during the same two years wielding an axe and saw to cut back plants, cut out dead wood and thinning-out the aged nurseries still containing plants set 3ft apart, but now 15ft high! By then they had also started to propagate, by both layers and cuttings, those plants that appeared to be on their last legs. In the same way, most of the plants that had been found a home at Tremeer were also propagated and returned to Lamellen. The restoration continued, with Daphne being responsible for most of the work, including the preparation of planting holes for the plants that began to arrive from the many gardening friends who wanted to provide help and en-couragement. Her only complaint was that 'one needed to be a mountain goat to get around the garden.' Sir Eric Savill visited the garden in 1963 with Dr Harold Fletcher, then Regius Keeper at RBG, Edinburgh, and upon seeing the half dozen nursery beds in the woods with plants spaced at 2ft apart, but now up to 15ft high, Dr Fletcher said 'Cut the whole lot down'. This advice was not taken too literally! Sir Eric sent a marvellous present of magnolias and large-leafed rhododendrons, which greatly encouraged Walter. Other early visitors included Alan Mitchell, Chris Page and Keith Rushforth. Keith sent plants and also seed from his later expeditions, whilst Walter continued to collect rhododendron plants and varieties of *Nothofagus* trees.

Walter continued to commute weekly to London and latterly rose to be Assistant Secretary at the Department of Trade and Industry, prior to retirement in 1971. Gradually, many of the main areas of the garden were brought back to their original splendour, but sadly, Daphne passed away a year later at the young age of 56, having spent a decade restoring the house and garden. Walter continued to be tireless in retirement, becoming Editor of the RHS Rhododendron and Camellia Yearbook (1974–82), Chairman of the RHS

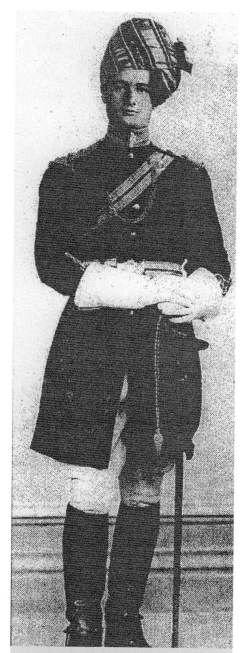

WALTER MAGOR, resplendent in his Indian Army uniform
FROM HIS OBITUARY IN THE TIMES MAY 24, 1995

JEREMY & FELICITY PETER-HOBLYN the current custodians of Lamellen

LAMELLEN ESTATE RECORDS

Rhododendron and Camellia Group (1976–80), President of the Cornwall Garden Society (1981–84) and was active in many other fields, including High Sheriff of Cornwall (1981). His enthusiasm for horticulture was infectious and he pursued his gardening interests in the same benevolent way as his father, and many major gardens in Great Britain and Ireland have reason to be grateful for the help and advice he provided. Many visiting gardeners benefited from Walter's generosity. 'I hope you will find room for these' he would say as he gave them a gift of well rooted cuttings, or even larger specimens of rare and unusual shrubs, when it was time to leave.[10]

Even enthusiastic, tireless horticulturalists eventually get old, so Felicity, Walter's eldest daughter, came to live at Lamellen in 1974 with her husband Jeremy Deeble Peter-Hoblyn, another Cornishman. Jeremy has an engineering background and, prior to retirement, was Chief Executive of a USA-based company, which involved a great deal of travelling, which left Felicity to run the garden. However, with the aid of a 'yellow digger', Jeremy constructed a network of paths that radiate at various levels from the vicinity of the House or the upper Main Drive. Accessible on foot, or by a small tractor, the paths have made the transport of materials and plants much easier, and it is no longer necessary to possess the sure-footedness of a 'mountain goat' to get around the garden.

Since 1975 most of the early shelter-belt plantings, principally *Pinus radiata,* have been replaced and new shelter-belts added. Other significant milestones have been the installation of a watering system throughout the garden, the introduction in 1989 of a propagation unit for both cuttings and seed, the ponds have been repaired and part of the banks of the stream have been reconstructed. Walter was awarded the RHS Veitch Memorial Medal in 1986, and whilst a keen and successful exhibitor at the shows, he still found time to encourage and help beginners with their entries.

In June 1991, upon reaching 80, he retired from an active involvement in the RCM Group, although he continued to take an interest in the Group's yearbook. He passed away on 1st May 1995 aged 83, leaving Felicity and Jeremy to continue what has been a labour of love in restoring Lamellen.

The areas due west, and at the back of the House, were never part of the garden, so the jungle of laurel and mature *Ilex* have been cleared and a new shelter-belt planted which has extended the garden around the House. Felicity and Jeremy managed to considerably increase the rate of new mixed plantings during the period 1987–2000, including many *Acer, Cornus, Sorbus, Prunus* and others. In the same timeframe a large collection of 150 species and hybrid magnolias has been established, together with the addition of 150 species and numerous hybrid rhododendrons.[6]

Jeremy retired in 2004 and, with the children all married, he and Felicity renovated and moved into the old barn, leaving Lamellen House available for family gatherings or for holiday lettings.

A new propagation unit has now been built and once again seed is being raised (mainly from Keith Rushforth) and cuttings reared; so the collections continue to be added to most years. Currently the North side slope is being substantially cleared of over-mature *Pinus radiata,* and all paths are now negotiable on a four-wheel-drive 'gator'.

So, Jeremy and Felicity are still able to get around and the garden continues to flourish in the care of the very knowledgeable and capable third-generation of the Magor Family, whilst their son, Edward, has recently become interested in the garden – excellent news in terms of securing Lamellen's future.

family documents from the Lamellen Estate records during research work to unravel a number of aspects relating to EJP Magor, EWM Magor and the development of the garden.

ACKNOWLEDGMENTS
The author is particularly grateful to Jeremy and Felicity Peter-Hoblyn who have unstintingly responded to queries and provided access to fragile ledgers and old

John Hammond

is a garden historian and long standing member of the RCM Group and was Director at Large for the American Rhododendron Society for many years

REFERENCES & NOTES ■ 1. As noted by Professor Anthony Charles Thomas, historian and archaeologist, Professor of Cornish Studies at Exeter University and Director of the Institute of Cornish Studies.   2. Tankin (1739). *History of Redruth.*   3. Cornwall Census 1851, 1861, 1871, 1881 & 1891. Civil Parishes of Redruth, Helland and St.Mabyn.   4. The origin of the massive R. 'Cornish Early Red', which is such a feature of many of the old Cornish gardens, is somewhat subjective. Some records suggest it is a synonym of R. 'Russellianum' (*catawbiense × arboreum*), a cross made at Russell's Nursery at Battersea, but this form is not very common in Cornwall. The more probable origin of R. 'Cornish Early Red' in Cornish gardens (which is not identical, but has a passing resemblance to R. 'Smithii') is another (*arboreum × ponticum*) cross, R. 'Rendall's Scarlet', made at Rendall's Nursery at St. Austell, Cornwall. The plants at Lamellen would have almost certainly been obtained from a nursery in Cornwall or Devon, and the records suggest they were supplied as R. 'Russellianum'.   5. Hammond, John M (2003). Tremeer Garden, St. Tudy, Cornwall. *World of the Rhododendron : Newsletter, Scottish Rhododendron Society,* 56, Spring 2003. 6. Peter-Hoblyn, Felicity, & Jeremy (2002). Lamellen 2002. Unpublished document. 7. Burns, Frances Scharen (2001). *To Have a Friend. An Exchange of Letters on Rhododendrons, Iris, Lilies, War and Peace 1945–1951. Del & Rae James and C. P. Raffill*. Big Rock Press, Vida, OR.   8. Dale, Bill (2000–2003). Correspondence with the author and copies of articles about the life of George Fraser.   9. Henny, Rudolph (1960). Five Letters From James Barto to Joseph Gable. *Quart. Bull. Amer. Rhod. Soc.* 14 (4): 220–231.   10. Gilbert, Richard (1995). Major Walter Moyle Magor, C.M.G, O.B.E., D.L. *Bulletin,* R.C. & M. Group. December, 1995.   11. James, Del (1950). James E. Barto. *Quart. Bull. Amer. Rhod. Soc.* 4 (2): 60-63. 12. Magor, Edward John Penberthy. 1901–1941. Lamellen Estate records, including ledgers, scrapbooks, old family documents and photographs.   13. Magor, Walter (1985). Lamellen. *Cornish Garden.* March1985: 14–19.   14. Magor, EJP (1916–1923). Notes From Lamellen. *The Rhododendron Society Notes.* East Bergholt, Suffolk.   15. Phillips, CE Lucas & Barber, Peter N (1967). *The Rothschild Rhododendrons.* Cassell & Co. Ltd, London.   16. Hammond, John M (2004). Mr. Magor and the North American Triangle : An Historical Perspective. *Journal, American Rhododendron Society.* 58 (3):135–148.   17. Phetteplace, Carl H (1961). The life and Work of James Barto. *Quart. Bull. Amer. Rhod. Soc.* 14(2):66–73. 14(3) 147–153. 18. Shephard, Sue (2003). *Seeds of Fortune, a Gardening Dynasty.* Bloomsbury, London. 19. *The Register Guard,* 1987–2003. Obituary & deaths archives. Eugene, Oregon. 20. Holms, John A (1919–1929). Himalayan and other Rhododendrons planted at Formakin, Bishopton, Renfrewshire and Larachmhor, Arisaig. Formakin Estate Records.   21. Livingston, Philip A, & West, Franklin H (eds)(1978). *Hybrids and Hybridizers.* Harrowood Books, Newtown Square, Pennsylvania.   22. Briggs, Roy W (1993). *'Chinese Wilson': A life of Ernest H, Wilson 1876–1930.* HMSO, London.   23. Pioneer Achievement Award : Edward John Penberthy Magor. *Journal, American Rhododendron Society.* 65(3): p146.

Gustave Croux, a forgotten French Rhododendron pioneer

PER M JØRGENSEN & DANIEL DUCROCQ

R. 'MONSIEUR MARCEL MÉNARD' flowering at the Arboretum, Milde, Norway in 2009

TERHI POUSI

WHILE MOST OF THE EARLY rhododendron history is centred in the British Isles (Postan 1996), there are a few continental exceptions, the most well-known being Germany (e.g. the Seidel dynasty, Schmalscheidt 1996).

Very little has been written about the French rhododendrons, and these plants have undoubtedly been less popular there. This is surprising since it was French missionaries (David, Delavay, Fargés and Soulié, to mention the most important) who first encountered the wealth of species in Yunnan and Tibet when, from about 1850, the French entered the region from Indochina. However, they sent mostly herbarium specimens back to Paris which were used by Adrien Franchet (1834–1900) when he described new species. It is known, however, that Delavay, at least, also sent seeds, which were grown in the Jardin des Plantes in central Paris, but they evidently disliked the conditions there or were wrongly treated (as stove plants) so they died before coming into use for further breeding.

Northwestern parts of France in particular, have a climate most suitable for rhododendrons and also acid soils, so this genus certainly was (and still is) used in gardening there as they became available, but very few French-bred cultivars are known.

Only recently we became aware of a very fine one, *Rhododendron* 'Monsieur Marcel Ménard', which is still in commerce and proved to be bred by Gustave Croux. On seeking information about its origin from the Rhododendron Register held by the Royal Horticultural Society, Alan Leslie, the International Rhododendron Registrar, provided us with a long list of other names registered with Croux as a breeder. He most evidently was a prolific hybridizer.

GUSTAVE CROUX HIS FAMILY AND NURSERY

Gustave Croux was born in 1848 in Chevilly-Larue , not far from Paris, into a family who had been gardeners since 1697. He was christened Gustave Louis, but appears mostly to have dropped the second name, so we call him Gustave in this article.

His father Jean Gabriel Croux (1817–1883) had established a nursery in Vallée d'Aulnay from the 1860s. Jean Gabriel had gradually enlarged the nursery by buying properties in the vicinity of Châtenay-Malabry, and in 1857 finally managed to acquire a most important piece of land from the Duchess de Giradin. It was here he erected his 'Villa de Glycine' where he lived with his family from 1862.

Jean Gabriel developed the nursery into one of international importance, as well as developing the park locally. Right from the beginning he was particularly keen on plants, especially trees and bushes, suitable for acidic soil. The catalogue of 1867 contained no less than 200 different rhododendrons.

In 1879, after he was made knight of 'Légion d' honneur' (in 1878) and his son Gustave (1848–1921) had married, he handed the business over to him.

Gustave took over a well-established firm which had received gold medals at several exhibitions – in 1878 two 'Grand Prix' at the Universal Exposition in Paris, and more importantly the great gold medal of the Czar at the first exhibition in St Petersburg (1869).

Gustave enlarged the activities and had over 100 employees at the end of the century. His policy was to present new cultivars which could be used in modern gardens and he therefore engaged in breeding of perennials, lilacs, roses and rhododendrons, and he liked to introduce plants new for French gardens. He even took his firm across the Atlantic to the US where he participated successfully at exhibitions in New Orleans (1884–85), Chicago (1893) and finally St Louis (1904)

GUSTAVE CROUX relaxing in a chair in 1878
COURTESY OF PÉPINIÈRES CROUX

From 1903 his only son Robert (1882–1918) joined in the running of the firm and took over completely after his marriage in 1911. However, he was killed in battle during the First World War and his widow took over until she died following an accident in 1926. Her mother, Mme Delehelle, then took charge until her grandsons. Maurice and Ubald. became of age.

Maurice took over in 1935 and in 1960 bought a farm near Génouilly, about 10 km North of Melun, where the nursery is now situated and still active under the leadership of his son Emmanuel.

CROUX'S RHODODENDRONS

It has not been possible fully to establish how, why and when Gustave started his breeding, since the archives and protocols were lost (in a fire). There is, however, reason to believe that Gustave, as an internationally oriented nurseryman with an interest in woody plants growing on acidic soils, became aware of the British cultivars being launched at that time, and got these to his nursery, evidenced by the surviving catalogues. He apparently started to breed based on that material. In 1890 he bought more land to expand the activities and we believe that it was about that

THE NURSERY OF CROUX IN CHATENAY-MALBARY, at its peak in 1893

time his breeding programme started. This is further supported by the first cultivars being registered in the Rhododendron Register shortly after the turn of the century (1902).

He obviously had success with his attempts, as several of his new cultivars were well received and won 'Cértificat de Mérite de la Société Nationale d'Horticulture de France', a French parallel to the awards given by the RHS in Britain. We have found eight cultivars of his given that award : R. 'Charles Prince', R. 'Docteur Léon Aurousseau', R. 'Jean Mercier', R. 'Louis Sébline', R. 'Madame André Panet', R. 'Madame Gustave Croux', R. 'Marcel Ménard', and R. 'Maurice Croux'. R. 'Marcel Ménard' is the only deep violet that he named, although there are a few others (most of them are red) in the list of 1933–34, where the rhododendrons are declared to be 'grand spécialité'.

Of these, only R. 'Marcel Ménard' still appears to be commercially available. It was actually registered as R. 'Monsieur Marcel Ménard' (in 1924) and named in memory of a school-friend of the breeder, but even the firm Croux dropped the 'Monsieur' in their catalogue. As pointed out by Kenneth Cox (2005) it is becoming more popular at the moment, and rightly so according to our experience. The flowers which are freely produced, somewhat resemble R. 'Purple Splendour', but are smaller, but the plant is healthier, less tall and denser, with good foliage; apparently a better garden plant, although the flowers are not quite as stunning.

It is not easy to understand why this is the only one of his many cultivars which have survived. There are some Croux azaleas still available, of which we know nothing, but they were made by his grandson Maurice, who also bred some rhododendrons.

ACKNOWLEDGEMENTS
We are most obliged to Marco Martella, Arboretum de la Vallée-aux-Loups for all the data which he has made available to us, and to Dr Alan Leslie, International Rhododendron Registrar at RHS Garden Wisley, for information from the International Rhododendron Register.

LTERATURE ■ André, ME (1885). Rapport au nom d'une commission sur les pépinière Croux & fils. Journ. Soc. Natl. Centr. d'Horticulture: 416–430. Cox, K (2005). Rhododendrons and Azaleas. A colour guide, Crowood Press. Croux, E (2010). Le famille Croux. Jardin de France, Mars–Avril: 44–47. Perpiniere Croux fils (1933–34). Catalogue générale, Rennes–Paris. Postan, C. (ed.) (1996). The Rhododendron Story, RHS. Schmalscheidt, W (1996). Hybrids for cold climates: The Seidels, in The Rhododendron Story: 109–114, RHS.

Per M Jørgensen & Daniel Ducrocq

both have an interest in the history of horticulture and work at the Arboretum and University Botanic Gardens at Milde near Bergen, Norway
Per M Jørgensen is Professor of Taxonomic Botany and has been responsible for establishing the rhododendron collection there, while Daniel Ducrocq is educated in agronomy, and is a gardener in the rose collection

CATALOGUE GÉNÉRAL

Des PÉPINIÈRES du VAL D'AULNAY

J. G. CROUX ✱ (1817–1883), G. L. CROUX O. ✱, ✿, ✚, ✚ (1848–1921), R. CROUX ✱, ✚, Ing. Agronome (1882–1918) Mort pour la France.

CROUX FILS

CHATENAY-MALABRY (Seine)

CULTURE GÉNÉRALE

DE

TOUS LES VÉGÉTAUX RUSTIQUES EN PLEIN AIR

FRUITIERS ET D'ORNEMENT

EN SUJETS DE TOUTES FORCES

1933-1934

Poste : CHATENAY-MALABRY (Seine).
Télégraphe : CROUX-CHATENAY-MALABRY (Seine).
Téléphone : CHATENAY-MALABRY (Seine) n° 406.
Gare : SCEAUX-ROBINSON (1.500 mètres).
Automobile : ITINÉRAIRE au dos du Catalogue.

Dépôt de ce Catalogue a été effectué conformément à la loi du 21 Octobre 1814.
Toute reproduction des Textes, Dessins et Photogravures est absolument interdite.

IMPRIMERIE OBERTHUR, RENNES-PARIS

FROM THE CATALOGUE OF CROUX 1933–34
Front page with all the owners through the years listed with their honours and recording Robert's death in action

Rhododendron multicolor MIQ: the spectacular red-flowered form rediscovered

WIGUNA RAHMAN, GEORGE ARGENT, TONY CONLON & NICKY SHARP

RHODODENDRON MULTICOLOR MIQ. was first described in 1860 from a collection attributed by Professor Sleumer to the Dutch horticulturist and botanist Johannes Teysmann (No778) from Mt Singalang on the west coast of Sumatra, Indonesia. The type specimen in Utrecht (The Netherlands) is without date or collector but is most likely to have been collected between 16 February and 5 March 1856, according to Teysmann's collecting itineraries (Steenis, 1950). The flowers were described on the label as *'coroll alb & sulphur'* and confirm the pale yellow flowers of the plants seen in cultivation since the 1960s (Argent, 2006). What has frustrated Vireya enthusiasts has been the lack of any sign of the red form grown at Veitch's 'Royal Exotic Nursery' on the Kings Road, Chelsea, London, from a collection of Charles Curtis. This flowered in cultivation for the first time on 2 November 1883 and was illustrated in *Curtis's Botanical Magazine* (Hooker, 1884) and in the *Florist & Pomologist* in the same year by the famous botanical artist WH Fitch (T Moore, 1884). Moore quotes from a communication from James Veitch and sons: *'The plant is of free growth and exceedingly floriferous, every shoot terminating in a truss of from four to seven brilliant scarlet-crimson flowers, which are produced continuously for several consecutive months. We consider this Rhododendron one of the most useful for the intermediate house ever introduced.'* This red form received a First Class Certificate of merit from the Royal Horticultural Society on 13 November 1883. It was one of only six Vireya species used by Veitch's nursery to produce the many hundreds of *'javanico-jasminiflorum'* hybrids towards the end of the 19th century and which caused such a sensation when exhibited in Victorian Britain.

The present plant was collected by Agus Suhatman (now Head of Ex-situ Conservation Division of Cibodas Botanic Garden) on an expedition in September 2006 to Bengkulu, South West Sumatra, on the summit of Mt Kaba

THE RED AND YELLOW COLOUR FORMS OF
RHODODENDRON MULTICOLOR
from the Fitch illustration in Curtis's Botanical Magazine, (Hooker, 1884)

(1490m asl). It was found on an open area of rocky hills dominated by *Melastoma malabathricum* L. It is now grown in the Cibodas Botanic Garden, Java, in front of the guest house. Here it is in a very exposed position which probably accounts for the deep red colouration of the foliage but it is growing strongly and showed signs (February 2011) of continuous flowering, as reported by James

RHODODENDRON MULTICOLOR in the Cibodas Botanic Garden, Western Java, showing the deep colouration of the foliage

WIGUNA RAHMAN

ACKNOWLEDGEMENTS
With thanks to Dr Mustaid Siregar and Dr Didik Widyatmoko, directors of the Bogor and Cibodas Botanic gardens respectively, who gave permission and support for the visit to Indonesia by the British authors. Financial support for this visit was given by The Royal Botanic Garden Edinburgh, The Royal Horticultural Society's Bursaries Committee, The Eve Bennett Trust and Kew Guild Awards. Thanks also to Graham Hardy for his willing and helpful library research and Kew librarians Julia Buckley and Lizbeth Gale for finding the 'Fitch' illustration for us.

Veitch, with flower buds, open flowers and fruit capsules in various states of maturation all on the same plant. It is quite possible that this recent collection is from the same or a very similar locality to that where Curtis collected his specimens. Bengkulu (then Bencoolen) was very accessible in Curtis's time but he never published his precise itineraries, to protect his finds from competitors, although he is known to have visited Sumatra on his early 1880–82 expedition on behalf of the Veitch nurseries (Steenis, 1950).

Cibodas Botanic Garden is located on the northern slope of Mount Gede-Pangrango, in Western Java at 1300–1425m asl. Annual rainfall is up to 3380mm/year. In this garden, *R. multicolor* blooms several times a year, with the peak season being December–January. In its peak blooming season, each plant can produce up to 30 inflorescences in various stages of development. The flower longevity is 8±3 days. While bud-burst to flower opening, male phase (opened flower to anther dehiscence), and female phase (days where the stigma becomes sticky and receptive, to corolla drop) are 3±3, 4±2, and 4±4 days, respectively. The inflorescence width is up to 9.69 cm when fully expanded.

Although *R. multicolor* is a Sumatran plant, in the Cibodas garden it shares the native pollinator (*Bombus rupifes* Lep.) with the native *R. javanicum* (Blume) Benn. and about 76% of open flowers develop into mature fruit.

REFERENCES & NOTES ■ Argent, G (2006). *Rhododendrons of Subgenus Vireya*. The Royal Horticultural Society & Royal Botanic Garden Edinburgh 1–388. Hooker, JD (1884). *Curtis's Botanical Magazine*, 40: (3rd Series), Tab. 6769. Moore, T (1884). *Florist and Pomologist* 112– 113. Steenis, CGGJ van (Ed) (1950). *Flora Malesiana* Series I, 1: 1–639.

Wiguna Rahman SP

is a scientist at the Cibodas Botanic Garden, LIPI, Siindanglaya, Cipanas, Cianjur 43253 PO. Box 19 SDL,

George Argent

is a Research Associate at the Royal Botanic Garden Edinburgh

Tony Conlon

is horticulturist in charge of the Vireya collection at the Royal Botanic Garden Edinburgh

Nicky Sharp

is supervisor of the botanical type specimen digitising project for the Mellon Foundation at the Royal Botanic Garden Edinburgh

W. H. Fitch. Del.

Chromolith. C. Severeyns. Brussels.

Rhododendron Curtisii.

REPRODUCTION OF THE 'FITCH' PAINTING OF THE RED FORM OF *RHODODENDRON MULTICOLOR*
(as *R. curtisii*) from *The Florist and Pomologist and Suburban Gardener,* (Thomas Moore, 1884)

Current taxonomy: hybrid zones in *Rhododendron* subsection Taliensia

TOBIAS MARCZEWSKI

AS AN INTRODUCTION TO THE READER I would first like to discuss some basic concepts of taxonomy, highlighting changes in our understanding of species and their evolutionary relationships since the emergence of techniques based on genetic data. Afterwards I will introduce some unanswered questions, and discuss how taxonomic problems experienced within the genus *Rhododendron* relate to these.

Before the availability of molecular methods, which use genomic information directly, all described species were based on morphological (visible) characters. To avoid any misconception I immediately want to point out that the appearance of a plant is still one of the most important considerations when attributing it to a species. However, the additional insights we can obtain from genetic methods allow us to test and refine these groupings. The main reasons are that we can minimise subjective choice of characters, and we much better understand the mechanisms leading to change in a simple molecule as DNA than to the potentially complex and incomparable differences between morphological characters. Because the mechanism of change in the genome can be considered the same for every genetic marker, we do not have to weigh them, or consider one more important than the other. This allows the combination of a multitude of markers to infer the relationship of species based on the number of genetic changes between them. Using some refined statistics to account for noise in the data, this approach is nowadays widely used to reconstruct the evolutionary relationships of species and depict them in phylogenetic trees. One important assumption about the evolutionary process implied in models used to infer relationships is that no characters (genes) are being exchanged between species at any time. Here, one of the most important definitions of a species becomes apparent: members of one species should not be able to produce offspring by mating with individuals of another species. In other words, species should be reproductively isolated, otherwise characters could be transferred between lineages and do not necessarily trace back to a common ancestor. The implication is that characteristics can only be exchanged (and homogenised) within one species, and newly arising characters will not leave the continuum of this species, although they can be passed on to descendants. After a long enough time, species that are reproductively isolated from each other are therefore expected to differ in several characteristics.

The theory regarding the divergence and evolution of species *after* they have attained reproductive isolation is reasonably well understood. However, we have yet to understand why and when most species attain reproductive isolation, and how they retain their integrity before this stage is reached. In some cases it is plausible that we witness only a temporary split, which will not proceed to the next step of speciation, but will instead result in two 'species' merging. To advance our understanding of the evolutionary process, and hence to elucidate forces that shaped present day diversity on our planet, it is crucial to investigate the dynamics of early stages of speciation, especially the stage during which species seem to be not completely isolated from each other.

Although most extant species seem to be reproductively isolated from each other, about 25% of plant species have been reported to form hybrids; understanding the reasons and implications of this violation of the criterion of reproductive isolation will help us to elucidate species relationships in more complex settings. Hybrid zones can be regarded as situations where the genomes of two species directly interact with each other, and investigating their composition and dynamics can help us to untangle the different forces leading to incompatibilities and finally fully isolated species.

As might be expected, the lack of reproductive isolation seems to be especially pronounced in young species that are not separated by long divergence times. In the genus *Rhododendron* this has the effect that phylogenetic methods have proved useful in clarifying the placement of subgenera, and to a certain extent subsections; the resolution on lower taxonomical levels, e.g. within subsections, is, however poor to non-existent. Clarifying relationships in subgenus Hymenanthes additionally poses problems, because its diversity is likely to have originated from a radiation event coinciding with the beginning of the last uplift phase of the Himalayas, approximately four million years ago. This leads to a high proportion of shared ancestral characters, and due to the problems mentioned previously regarding the choice of morphological characters, this often results in the description of controversial species and varieties, along with uncertainty regarding their relationships. While this complicates taxonomy in the complex, it offers us the exciting opportunity to investigate evolutionary dynamics at this crucial stage of species divergence.

PHD PROJECT

Subsection *Taliensia* in subgenus Hymenanthes comprises several closely related species, and as David Chamberlain noted in his 1982 revision (p333), an especially complex group of species around *Rhododendron taliense*, *R. roxieanum*, *R. alutaceum*, *R. phaeochrysum* and *R. aganniphum* exists. For many species good, qualitative, morphological characters are lacking so that the characters that have been used to delimit species have been mostly leaf shape and hair types, especially the indumentum (hairs on the underside of leaves). However, several described varieties of these species appear morphologically intermediate between certain members of the complex, and are potentially hybrids or of hybrid origin. After initial assessment in the field in 2007, two species pairs of subsection Taliensia, including their varieties, were chosen for more detailed investigation. First, *R. roxieanum* and *R. clementinae*, focusing on *R. roxieanum* var. *cucullatum*, which shows morphological tendencies towards *R. clementinae*. Second, *R. aganniphum* and *R.*

phaeochrysum, as individuals of *R. aganniphum* var. *flavorufum* were occurring amongst plants in a hybrid swarm between the two species. Due to the taxonomical focus of previous research in *Rhododendron*, population sampling is generally lacking, and consequently the variability of characters within populations is unknown. At the beginning of the project it was therefore crucial to obtain population samples, to identify groups of individuals inside these taxonomically difficult complexes that actually behave as continua. In this context 'continua' means groups within these complexes that share a common genepool and can therefore be considered species. Morphology generally points us in the right direction, but the morphological groups obtained have to be confirmed, or refined, employing genetic methods. The advantage of a population genetic approach is not only that it enables us to assess variability within the groups in question, but additionally allows us to estimate the extent of cross-species geneflow where species co-occur. With this data we can determine the possible

Fig 1. **MAP SHOWING SAMPLE LOCALITIES OF POPULATIONS**

impact of geneflow on genetic composition in local populations, and investigate the coherence of a species in a geographical setting. After the delimitation of species, hybrid zones can then be used to investigate the factors that separate the species. For both species pairs, population samples were obtained at a location where they co-occur (sympatric) along with morphological intermediates found at the site. Furthermore, for each of the four species a reference population was obtained elsewhere to estimate population divergence within species.

All four species investigated occur exclusively in South-West China, mainly in the provinces of Yunnan and Sichuan (Fig 1), and are restricted to altitudes above 3000m. Therefore the distribution of populations is patchy, restricted to mountain ranges and inselbergs. Due to limited geneflow between populations of the same species that are separated by geology, together with lacking reproductive barriers, this could lead to sympatric populations of different species sharing more genes than different populations of the same species, indicating local merging of groups. The genetic analysis carried out using a method called AFLP revealed that this is not the case, as all species are considerably more differentiated than populations of the same species. Local geneflow therefore does not seem to impact on overall species identity.

R. ROXIEANUM – R. CLEMENTINAE

Populations for this species pair were collected on Lao Jun Shan, Shika Shan, and Haba Shan. The species are morphologically distinct: *R. clementinae*, for example, has much broader leaves than *R. roxieanum* (Fig 2) and seems to prefer higher altitudes. However, at Lao Jun Shan, *R. roxieanum* var. *cucullatum* shows morphological tendencies towards *R. clementinae*: significantly broader leaves, longer indumentum hairs, and a preference for '*clementinae* altitudes', along with plants occasionally exhibiting typical hybrid characteristics such as rugose leaves. Furthermore, *R. roxieanum*, and hence one or both of its varieties, is likely to be involved in the controversial complex of varieties around *R. alutaceum*, making a clarification of the status of its varieties desirable.

On Lao Jun Shan both species grow in sympatry, at altitudes between 3700 and 4000m. At the lower limit of this range only *R. roxieanum* var. *roxieanum* can be found, while the upper limit is dominated by *R. clementinae*.

Fig 2. **LEAF & INDUMENTUM MORPHOLOGY OF *RHODODENDRON CLEMENTINAE* & *R. ROXIEANUM*** A) R. clementinae; large broad leaves, indumentum hairs long and densely compacted. B, C) *R. roxieanum* var. *cucullatum*; leaves wider than *R. roxieanum* var. *roxieanum*, but narrower than *R. clementinae*; indumentum not compacted but often thicker than in *R. roxieanum* var. *roxieanum*; D) *R. roxieanum* var. *roxieanum*; very narrow to linear leaves, indumentum hairs of medium length, not compacted.

Fig 3. **INDUMENTUM MORPHOLOGY OF *RHODODENDRON AGANNIPHUM* & *R. PHAEOCHRYSUM***
A) *R. aganniphum* var. *aganniphum*; indumentum remains white at maturity, long hairs, never splitting.
B, C) Forms close to A; indumentum starts splitting at maturity but remains more or less white (B) or
slightly changes colour (C). **D)** *R. aganniphum* var. *flavorufum*; indumentum with slightly shorter hairs,
splitting in medium aged leaves, becoming patchy in maturity and turning deep brown. **E)** Forms close to
F; indumentum with hairs visibly shorter than D, becoming patchy early, then later partly or entirely
appearing agglutinated. **F)** *R. phaeochrysum*; indumentum turns dark red-brown at maturity, short hairs,
cannot split due to missing longer hairs.

From about 3800m onwards the two species co-occur, *R. roxieanum* var. *roxieanum* becoming less frequent as *R. roxieanum* var. *cucullatum* becomes more abundant. While large homogeneous stands of *R. roxieanum* var. *roxieanum* can be found below 3800m, the plants encountered higher up are mostly solitary, contrasting with some large stands of *R. roxieanum* var. *cucullatum*.

Genetic fingerprinting confirmed one hybrid between *R. clementinae* and *R. roxieanum*, providing evidence that the two species do hybridise, but apparently at a lower rate than expected. Furthermore, *R. roxieanum* var. *cucullatum* is not significantly diverged from *R. roxieanum* var. *roxieanum*, indicating that according to current data the status as a variety is best maintained. However, an additionally carried out analysis of leaf wax composition, which is based on differences in the *n*-alkane profile, pointed to an affinity of *R. roxieanum* var. *cucullatum* to *R. clementinae*. This suggests a potential historic hybridisation event, and depending how far in the past this event occurred, it will not be detected easily with available genetic methods.

R. AGANNIPHUM – R. PHAEOCHRYSUM

Several differing population settings were obtained for this species pair. First, on Baima Shan populations were sampled where both species occur sympatrically, forming a swarm of intermediates with varying morphology, including *R. aganniphum* var. *flavorufum* (Fig 3). Second, on top of Baima Shan a population of individuals with intermediate but homogeneous morphology was encountered and sampled. Last, the sampled reference populations for both species were growing sympatrically on Dáxu Shan, but no intermediates occurred here. Therefore, the following settings were encountered: two hybrid populations with differing morphology; two contrasting sympatric population settings, one in which intermediates could be found, and another where the species were apparently coexisting without hybrids being formed.

As morphology indicated, most individuals of the sympatric reference populations on Dáxu Shan were genetically pure members of the respective species. However, there were a few exceptions to this. This indicates that although no hybridisation is occurring in the contemporary populations, parts of the genome have been transferred in the past, and furthermore, these individuals are morphologically not different from other members of the respective species. Caution is therefore advised when basing genetic analyses of species on single individuals, and it emphasises the importance of population sampling in the complex.

The genetic analysis of the two hybrid populations revealed that the homogeneous hybrid population comprises nearly entirely first generation hybrids (F1), while the swarm population, conforming to morphology, encompasses several backcross classes. Unexpectedly, the F1 hybrid is genetically identical to *R. phaeochrysum* var. *agglutinatum*. This shows how morphology can give crucial hints, and how genetic methods can help us to overcome subjective judgements, as to most observers *R. aganniphum* var. *flavorufum* might appear intermediate and would therefore be interpreted as the F1 hybrid; it is however a later generation backcross to *R. aganniphum*. When later generation backcrosses are not formed, as in the case of F1 dominated hybrid zones, no geneflow should occur between the species. Hence they are in effect reproductively isolated from each other. This is the case for the hybrid population on top of Baima Shan, but not for the swarm population. Differences between these two populations are difficult to identify, but environmental factors are likely to play an important role. Evidence of how species might retain their integrity despite geneflow is provided by genetic patterns observed in both hybrid populations. Most of the genome is apparently transmitted more or less freely between the two parental species, *R. aganniphum* and *R. phaeochrysum*, which are therefore not significantly differentiated for most genetic markers. However, certain parts of the genome are not transferred, even when hybrids are formed. It is likely that these parts are important for the identity of the species, and further research will hopefully be able to help us understand their function and

importance for the species. This reminds us that we still have a long and very exciting path ahead of us while unravelling the forces that have shaped these species, and continue to shape them.

ACKNOWLEDGEMENTS

As I have here the unique opportunity to reach most of the people that provided the much needed financial support for this project, I want to emphasise how thankful I am to all of the members of the RHS Rhododendron, Camellia and Magnolia Group that have contributed so kindly to the project fund, and made this research possible. Furthermore, I want to thank my supervisors, Mary Gibby, Richard Milne and David Chamberlain for their constant support and advice; Gao Lian-Ming and Liu Jie for their invaluable assistance during fieldwork; The Davis Expedition Fund for providing matching funding for the expedition in 2008, and David Rankin for guidance while carrying out the leaf wax analysis.

FURTHER READING

(2007). The Rhododendron, Camellia & Magnolia Group *Bulletin*. Number 95.

Chadwick, MD, DF Chamberlain, BA Knights, A McAleese, S Peters, DWH Rankin, and F Sanderson, (2000). Analysis of leaf waxes as a taxonomic guide to *Rhododendron* subsection Taliensia. *Annals of Botany* 86:371–384.

Chamberlain, D.F, (1982). A Revision of Rhododendron, II. Subgenus Hymenanthes. *Notes from the Royal Botanic Garden Edinburgh* 39(2):209–486.

Marczewski, T, (2011). Hybrid Zones in *Rhododendron* subsection Taliensia, PhD Thesis, University of Edinburgh.

Tobias Marczewski

gained a PhD from the University of Edinburgh in 2011 after completing this research project

Appreciation

Philip Tregunna 1931–2011

HEAD GARDENER CAERHAYS CASTLE 1956–1996

PHILIP TREGUNNA started work at Caerhays Castle Gardens aged 14. His first duties included opening the field gate on the way to the Kitchen Garden so that his elders and betters did not have to alight from their bicycles on the way to work, and then being tasked to remove weeds from the walls with a nail for days on end.

In 1956, at the age of 25, Philip was promoted to head gardener by my father. The garden staff had by then declined from 60 before the First War to around 10. His predecessor, Charles Michael, had noticed and promoted Philip's desire to learn the practicalities of how to propagate and hybridise the wealth of Asiatic plant species which had arrived at Caerhays from the Wilson and Forrest expeditions to Southern China between 1905 and 1932.

PHILIP TREGUNNA seen here with his wonderful *Magnolia* 'Caerhays Surprise', winner of the RHS Reginald Cory Memorial Cup

It is very unusual today for head gardeners not to have university degrees or at least several initials after their name. Philip, and his chosen successor as head gardener at Caerhays, Jaimie Parsons, give us ample proof that knowledge and learning can pass by word of mouth rather than necessarily in the classroom.

Philip was to preside over the full maturity of the original Asiatic plants and many of the early hybrids created by JC Williams (deceased 1939) and his son Charles Williams (deceased 1955) in the 1960s and 1970s. He was, however, not slow to make his own major contribution.

As early as 1959, Philip had the exceptional foresight to cross two magnolias which never normally flower within 2 months of each other. His hybrid between *Magnolia campbelli* ssp. *mollicomata* and *M. liliiflora* 'Nigra' first flowered in 1968. In 1973 it was awarded the RHS Reginald Cory Memorial Cup for the best new woody plant introduction of the year (a national and international award) as well as an

Award of Merit. As we now know, this was christened *Magnolia* 'Caerhays Surprise'. A magnolia for the smaller garden, a magnolia, not for places such as Caerhays, but for magnolia enthusiasts with space for only the odd plant and not just in the UK but, via New Zealand and Swiss growers, throughout the USA and Europe. How many tens of thousands of these plants will be enjoyed for generations to come – and all the work of one exceptionally talented hybridiser and propagator.

Philip and my father bred and raised scores of other magnolia hybrids in their 40 years together but they were generally dismissive of their achievements and wisely only named and registered a handful of the very best. Philip was the first to flower *Magnolia* 'Caerhays Belle'; the original of which can be viewed from the front door at Caerhays. *Magnolia* 'Kew's Surprise' was, despite its name, raised at Caerhays, where it first flowered in 1967 and subsequently received an FCC. My father (tongue in cheek) told the curator of Kew that it was one of the few good things to come from Kew and it was named accordingly. *Magnolia* 'J.C. Williams' (FCC 2002), a hybrid between *M. sargentiana* var. *robusta* and *M. sprengeri* 'Diva', was perhaps their darkest flowered and currently most popular creation. Of more recent origin is *Magnolia* 'F.J. Williams', named after my father, which is a very early flowering reddish-purple *sargentiana* var. *robusta* x *campbellii* ssp. *mollicomata* 'Lanarth' hybrid. This first flowered only a few years ago and received Philip's full commendation in his retirement.

Last but not least is *Magnolia* 'Philip Tregunna', a *M. sargentiana* var. *robusta* hybrid with *M. campbellii*. This too received an FCC in 1992. It is early flowering with exquisite clear pink upright cup-shaped flowers. Such words, as is often the case when trying to describe magnolia flowers, do it scant justice.

In the field of rhododendrons, Philip may be best remembered for the wonderful bright waxy yellow *cinnabarinum* x *concatenans* hybrid registered in 1966 and aptly named *R*. 'Caerhays Philip'. Sadly, the plants all died out at Caerhays in the 1980s as both parents were especially prone to mildew and rust attack. This is however a cross which can now be replicated.

Those of you who can remember back to Chelsea in the 1990s may recollect the naming of *R*. 'Tinners Blush' and *R*. 'High Sheriff' by Seb Coe. These were Philip's *decorum* x *williamsianum* hybrids.

Philip also raised a whole series of hybrids named after farms on the Caerhays estate. *R*. 'Penvose' (*tephropeplum* x *cinnabarinum*), *R*. 'Polgrain' (same cross), *R*. 'Rescassa' (*decorum* x *campylocarpum*), *R*. 'Treberrick' ('Moser's Maroon' x *griersonianum*) are perhaps the best known. Today each of the eight bedrooms at The Vean is named after one of these hybrids and each room features a picture of the farmhouse, the plant and its registration/award documents.

Other more difficult and exotic hybrids included the November flowering *R*. 'Winter Intruder' (*arboreum* ssp. *delavayi* x 'Nobleanum')

and range of scented rhododendrons for May. For every successfully named hybrid the garden still has huge clumps of 'not good enough'.

Turning to camellias, it was Philip who helped secure an AM for *Camellia* x *williamsii* 'Caerhays' (1967) and *C*. x *williamsii* 'George Blandford' (1974) – two of the later double x *williamsii* hybrids. There are many other x *williamsii* hybrids which have received similar recognition over the years.

I have no doubt that my father's passion and enthusiasm for gardening emanated directly from Philip's tuition. My father knew nothing at all about gardening when he inherited Caerhays in 1955 and I too was to grow up with the best possible horticultural grounding, although there were many pranks and much naughtiness along the way.

Perhaps the most astonishing thing about Philip's career as a gardener and horticulturalist was that his many brothers, sisters and huge family were flabbergasted to hear of his achievements, his role in the RHS and his frequent conducted tours of the gardens with the Queen Mother, Prince Charles and even Margaret Thatcher. Philip, in his own quiet and unassuming manner, had not deemed it necessary to tell them!

The wake was adorned with pictures of many of Philip's gardening friends: Harold and John Hillier, Frank Knight, Roy Lancaster, John Bond, Jim Gardiner – to mention just a few.

Loyalty and continuity, unfashionable though it may be today, is what a Cornish garden like Caerhays must have to prosper, develop and expand, while welcoming the public. Philip was and achieved all of these things while still finding a great deal of time in retirement to monitor and advise his successor. The many friends of Caerhays Gardens will miss him, but his enormous legacy lives on for all to enjoy. Great gardeners really do leave something behind!

Charles Williams

Notes from the International Rhododendron Registrar 2011

ALAN LESLIE

RHODODENDRON 'DENTELLE' is a newly registered azaleodendron bred from *periclymenoides* x 'Karen Triplett'   LILIANE & ALEX LE DUIGOU

IN THE FIRST PART OF MY NOTES last year I had anticipated the publication of the sixth supplement to *The International Rhododendron Register and Checklist* by the time those notes appeared in the Yearbook. Events did not work out as planned and the sixth supplement did not appear until the second half of 2011 and was then a combined list of the registrations for 2009 and 2010. We should now be back to a schedule of annual publications and these current notes cover registration activity for 2010 and up to October 2011. The 2010 list added a further 94 names to the Register and 2011 is already well ahead of this with 121 new names. The majority continue to be elepidote rhododendrons, but this year we have had an unusual number of azaleas (29), thanks in part to a large batch from the still burgeoning activity at the Hachmann Nursery in Germany, a set of *Rhododendron* 'Homebush' hybrids from Mrs Legrand in England, which are derived from the breeding work undertaken in the 1970s by her father, WGT Hyde, together with several more from Prof Kondratovičs at the Rhododendron Nursery Babīte of the University of Latvia.

Also listed amongst these azaleas are two new double-flowered seedlings raised by M.S. Viraraghavan, in southern India, which remarkably come from wild-collected seed of *R. simsii*, gathered by the Phu River, near Loei in Thailand in 1998 by Mr Thinakorn Komkris. *R.* 'Kodai Ruffles' and *R.* 'Kodai Fire' are dark reddish-pink and orange-red respectively, the former with very wavy-edged lobes. Mr Viraraghavan has also added to his set of "Palni" rhododendron cultivars, which derive in part from hybrids of *R. arboreum* ssp. *nilagiricum*, a native of southern India, which is a rarely listed parent in the Register records.

His *R.* 'Palni Sunrise' and *R.* 'Palni Fire' are, of course, both single-flowered, and new double-flowered rhododendron cultivars are very unusual. However, no less than five have been registered during the period under review: from Japan, Germany, Norway and New Zealand. A double form of *R. brachycarpum* was involved in the parentage of both Hideo Suzuki's *R.* 'Mone-hime' and Sentaro Kenke's *R.* 'Sen-no-izayoi', the latter getting an extra dose of "doubleness" from a double variant of *R. degronianum* ssp. *heptamerum* var. *kyomaruense*. In the case of *R.* 'June Gardiner', raised and named in New Zealand by Susan Davies, its semi-double character is derived from a double-flowered selection of *R. griffithianum*, in this case crossed with *R.* 'Lem's Cameo', to produce a flower that starts white, striped with pink, and ages to white. Wolfgang Reich's selection named after his late younger brother, *R.* 'Joachim Reich', is from 'Gletschernacht' x 'April Rose' and it is the latter cultivar that contributes the doubleness factor on this occasion. Finally we have *R.* 'Kari's Surprise' grown in Norway by Kari Grov, from seed sent by Jim Barlup in the USA and subsequently named and registered by Per Magnus Jørgensen. Its parentage is 'Fantastica' x 'Snow Candle', so in this case it is not apparent where the genetic trigger has come from to produce the petaloid

RHODODENDRON 'BEAU VALLON'

JEAN-FRANCOIS SAINT-JALM

stamens which adorn the centre of its uniformly pinkish-rose corollas.

There were few vireyas added to the list this time, but two of these did catch my eye during registration. Both were derived from *suaveolens* x 'Scentsation' and were raised by Brian Oldham in New Zealand. Unsurprisingly with that parentage, both *R.* 'Oldham's Theressa' and *R.* 'Lydia Ellen' are scented, the latter strongly so and this cultivar is also noted to be unusual, and useful, in being very long-lasting as a cut flower. *R.* 'Oldham's Theressa' (named for his daughter-in-law) is a very pretty pink and white bicolour – purplish pink lobes and a white tube – with the additional attraction of violet anthers.

Other cultivars that stood out, for reasons which I have to admit are pure personal prejudice, included two with unusual calyces: the elepidote cultivar *R.* 'Beau Vallon' and the azaleodendron *R.* 'Dentelle'. Both are new French cultivars, the former derived from 'Halopeanum' x 'September Song' and raised by Jean-Francois Saint-Jalm. After the purplish pink and pale yellow corollas have fallen the petaloid calyces remain and these are white, and like the corollas have conspicuous dark purplish red markings. The effect is rather startling. More restrained, but no less attractive, are the calyces in *R.* 'Dentelle', a rarity in itself in being a new azaleodendron cultivar. This was raised by Liliane and Alex Le Duigou and the calyx is up to 35mm long and divided very deeply into linear, white, strongly reflexed lobes. The tubular funnel-shaped corolla is pure white, opening from pale yellow and yellowish pink-tinged buds. It parentage is *periclymenoides* x 'Karen Triplett'.

Three American cultivars were amongst several that left a lasting impression for their sheer beauty: *R.* 'Violet Breeze' is a fairly complex elepidote hybrid from Jim Barlup and very pale purple in colour with just the narrowest margin of much darker purple, coupled with a good dark spotted blotch and white anthers; *R.* 'Martha Player' is a 'Mrs Sam' x *hyperythrum* hybrid, raised by Lonnie Player, with beautifully formed trusses of white flowers mostly prettily spotted with red, whilst *R.* 'Heritage Campfire Peach' is one of a series of plants, in this case of unknown parentage, originally hybridised by Jim Cowles in the 1960s, grown at the Heritage Museums and Gardens at Sandwich, Massachusetts and now registered by the Sandwich Club. It has tight trusses of broadly funnel-shaped flowers of the palest yellow-green, the broadly overlapping lobes suffused a soft purplish pink.

RHODODENDRON 'VIOLET BREEZE'   JIM BARLUP

RHODODENDRON 'TRIPLE A' © CHRISTINA WOODWARD

fact that the raiser's interest in the genus was first awakened when he lived in that country. R. 'Forbidden Plateau' takes us into quite different territory as this elepidote cultivar, raised by Harry Wright in British Columbia, Canada, is named after a feature visible from his property. The flowers open white and change to pink and recall the local legend about the plateau, to which in the past the local people sent their families to avoid frequent raids made upon their homes; on one occasion the men returned to the plateau to retrieve their women and children, but although they searched until it snowed there was no sign of them. When it did snow the snow began to change from white to red and the place was declared evil and forbidden. More prosaically, it is now suggested that this change of colour in the snow can be attributed to a chemical reaction between the snow and a particular moss growing in that area.

I have mentioned before the often curious and varied derivations that lie behind many cultivar epithets. There are some nice examples amongst these recent registrations: R. 'Triple A' is the name given to a *minus* x *impeditum* derivative raised by the late Dr Brueckner in Canada and commemorating his three grandchildren, all of whose first names begin with the letter A; R. 'Dathocarmapie' is a R. *cinnabarinum* hybrid raised in France by Marie Thérèse Bleuzen and is a composite of the names of her five grandchildren – Damien, Thomas, Carla, Malo and Pierre! Indeed grandchildren seem to be an influential source of nomenclature for rhododendron cultivars, for whilst Dr Brueckner's widow (Marta Brueckner) was reluctant to have a plant directly named after her, she did consent to the epithet R. 'Ayomi', a combination of the names "Ayo" and "Omi" which her grandchildren use for her. Mrs Legrand too has used the names of her four grandchildren for the set of R. 'Homebush' hybrid azaleas that were launched by Millais Nurseries at Chelsea Show in 2011 and which some of you may have seen on the television: R. 'Charlotte Megan', R. 'Helena Evelyn', R. 'Jessica Rose' and R. 'Thomas David'.

Another Brueckner plant, R. 'Aoteoroa', a Maori name for New Zealand and translating as "the land of the long white cloud", marks the

As I have explained previously, part of my role, beside the registration of new names, is to

RHODODENDRON 'AYOMI'

© CHRISTINA WOODWARD

try and track down information about all named cultivars and if necessary add entries for them to the Checklist element of the International Register and Checklist. Over the last two years I have been continuing actively to pursue data on German-raised cultivars and am pleased to report that entries for all Bernhard Knorr's 200 or more named cultivars and Groups have been added to the database. My thanks are due to him and in particular his friend Tijs Huisman, who has been acting as go-between for us, translating my queries into German and Mr Knorr's replies into English. I am delighted too to have received a substantial raft of new registrations compiled by Manuela Oppenrieder, which continue to chronicle the extensive breeding work undertaken both by the late Hans Hachmann and latterly by his son Holger. The Register is also now up to date with the significant number of new plants raised and named by Wolfgang Reich and I am still extracting new entries or additional information from the continuing correspondence and published works of Walter Schmalscheidt. I am indebted to Julia Westhoff for help in pursuing my enquiries with several other German breeders.

Amongst other sources of new information that have been extracted over the past year is a 1933–34 catalogue from the Croux Fils Nursery in Paris, which has considerably improved and expanded our account of Croux cultivars, and the latest version of Parker Smith's list of Californian-raised cultivars. The latter heralds a move next year to concentrate on dealing with a raft of outstanding queries and corrections relating to the Register and Checklist entries for North American-raised cultivars. At the same time I shall be seeking information on any other American-raised plants for which we, as yet, have no record.

RHODODENDRON '**CHARLOTTE MEGAN**'   DAVID MILLAIS

Whilst unfortunately I cannot yet report that we have the database online, some progress has been made towards this goal and this continues to be a firm commitment and target for the Society to achieve. However, I remain willing and able to provide electronic reports from the database to any enquirers. I am also happy to say that, thanks to the International Society for Horticultural Science, the most recent, eighth edition of the *International Code of Nomenclature for Cultivated Plants* (the 'Cultivated Plant Code'), is for the first time available to download, for no charge, from www.ishs.org/acta/. The Code guides us all in dealing with the formation and publication of new cultivar and Group names.

As ever, my thanks are due to the national registrars who all do so much to facilitate the registration process and field all too many queries from me. They are Jay Murray (North America), Ken Gillanders (Australia), Katsuhisa Fujiwara (Japan) and Brian Coker (New Zealand). Many of you will know that Brian was very badly injured in the Christchurch earthquake in 2011 and has shown tremendous courage and determination in trying to rebuild his life. I am sure all rhododendron enthusiasts will join me in wishing him all the best for the future.

Exceptional Plants 2011

Shows

GOOD PUBLIC ATTENDANCE AT THE MAIN RHODODENDRON COMPETITION AT ROSEMOOR
is one of the hallmarks of its continuing success   SALLY HAYWARD

ARRANGEMENTS FOR THE TWO London camellia shows seemed to work better in 2011 with the early competition taking place alongside the London Orchid Show and the main competition held more or less at its usual time. Working with the orchid community was very effective; surprisingly the two plant groups do seem to complement each other very well.

For the purposes of showing it did appear that we had a different cross-section of the public viewing the camellia blooms, and I suspect the orchid exhibitors benefited also to some degree. Sharing with the Orchid Show, however, failed to solve the seemingly intractable problem that still exists with respect to show timings and availability; it is proving impossible to generate a long enough period of time between the early and main competitions. This situation is tending to concentrate the varieties displayed. If a clear

month was allowed between them, I am sure we would see a wider range of varieties, however the opportunities to hold shows at the 'correct' times are increasingly scarce. As I have noted before, I think camellias have a secret communications system – a variety will decide for itself to have a good blooming year regardless of location or variations in the weather conditions – how can this be?

The cumulative effect of several non-conducive winters was really in evidence across both competitions. The more weather sensitive camellias tend to decline gradually over a number of seasons through die-back or simply a lack of growth and this decline was evidenced through the entries this year. Large and very large flowered *Camellia japonica* entries were clearly further reduced as these varieties do tend to be less resilient. This situation probably contributed to the apparent fewer number of varieties in general. Over the five years from around 2001 we saw an increasing number of *C. reticulata* hybrids being shown but these have also reduced back to the traditional forms with just the odd exception. This position is making the production of these notes even more challenging as repetition in varieties makes for repetition in the reports. For the early competition itself, without greenhouse grown plants the show would have been very poor; fortunately those who did show produced a very high quality (if not quantity) competition. The Main Camellia Competition was much better supported in terms of volume but oddly the quality was lower!

CAMELLIA JAPONICA 'ANN SOTHERN'

SALLY HAYWARD

CAMELLIA JAPONICA 'TAMMIA'

SALLY HAYWARD

VINCENT SQUARE

C. japonica '**Tammia**' Flowers with multi-coloured petals that are either edged or striped always seem popular – take one of the world's favourite camellias, *C. japonica* 'Margaret Davis', as an example. Consequently, it is odd why *C.* 'Tammia' is not growing as widely in the UK as it is overseas.

A small or miniature white formal double with pink edging to the petals; the plant is healthy and reliable, however I suspect its flaw

lies in a lack of flower. It is not a plant that covers itself in blooms in UK gardens; however, those that it does produce are almost always perfect examples.

I was advised to try the almost identical variety *C.* 'Grace Albritton' as a more floriferous alternative. Sadly, this proved not to be the case.

For best results with either of these varieties a warm spot with plenty of sun seems to be recommended, especially so as *C.* 'Tammia' seems very sun tolerant and resistant to scorching.

C. japonica '**Ann Sothern**' If you are looking for a plant to give a bold foliage statement in the garden whilst still having some flowering interest, *C.* 'Ann Sothern' may well be the answer and it is certainly a candidate for a "laurel killer". Large, very dark green leaves make this plant really stand out when not in flower – why grow a laurel? The flowers are a pastel pink with quite a range of colour through the life of the bloom, indeed the petals may shade lighter in tone towards the base with the whole flower taking on a much lighter shell pink tone occasionally as it matures. The stamens can be darker than ideal which may limit the plant as a show variety but as a garden plant it is excellent.

C. hybrid 'El Dorado' (*pitardii* x *japonica* 'Tiffany') Any hybrid of *C.* 'Tiffany' would surely produce something interesting, if not subtle, and *C.* 'El Dorado' is certainly an interesting plant and, what's more, a personal favourite of mine.

This 40+ year-old *C. pitardii* hybrid is an example of why we need to stop thinking of this class of plant as new or in some way unproven. They should be the backbone of any serious camellia collection as they are large flowered, tough and reliable, with a heavy and long blooming season.

C. 'El Dorado' has an unusual, loose peony form flower in a good shade of pink with a slightly ruffled edge. Unfortunately the older flowers, being so open, can look a little sad before they fall but this is only a minor demerit. If you have the space, try growing *C.* 'El Dorado' in a grouping of three with *C.* x *williamsii* 'Senorita' and *C.* 'Nicky Crisp' (another *C. pitardii* hybrid) – this would be a feature to raise the envy of any gardener.

CAMELLIA 'EL DORADO'

SALLY HAYWARD

C. japonica 'Doutor Balthazar de Mello' If a camellia stays popular over many years it will gain names as well as growth rings! This Portuguese variety is well over 100 years old and consequently has many names including 'Dr Balthazar de Milo' which it was shown under at the 2011 SW Branch Camellia Competition at Rosemoor. Carnation-mimicking fimbriated camellias are a novelty and when combined with stripes could be considered rather too much to live with. However, this variety, fimbriated white with red stripes still retains a degree of elegance.

As with all edged camellias it is necessary to watch the plants' tendency to revert to their non-fimbriated forms, as in the blink of an eye (5 years) the special plant will have disappeared.

CAMELLIA JAPONICA 'DOUTOR BALTHAZAR DE MELLO'

SALLY HAYWARD

C. japonica 'Madame Lebois' So if a 100 year-old camellia can gain a few names, how about one over 150. The Camellia Register lists over 10 alternative names or synonyms for this variety, so it must have been doing something well since illustrated by Verschaffelt in 1854 – incidentally, one of the better illustrations to my eye. A very regular formal double of a good cherry red, the petals lay perfectly on each other in a good bloom. However, in warmer climates more petals can appear, which may lead to an interesting spiral effect but more likely just cause the symmetry and best characteristics of the plant to be lost. If you are looking for a plant with a good pedigree for say an older garden but still want a modern feel to the flowers then *C.* 'Madame Lebois' is a good choice – if you can find it.

CAMELLIA JAPONICA 'MADAME LEBOIS'

SALLY HAYWARD

RHODODENDRON COELONEURON

SALLY HAYWARD

Following one of the coldest and most prolonged winters in living memory only two gardens managed to stage competitive exhibits at the 2011 Early Rhododendron Competition. How good, though, to welcome Tregothnan back to the Vincent Square benches after so many years.

Both the Tregothnan and Exbury Estates have the benefit of being situated relatively close to the coast and the quality of the blooms they brought to the show benches earned envious glances from those of us who garden inland and had lost not only that season's flower buds but often mature plants to the ravages of the exceptional weather.

A very fine truss of **Rhododendron coeloneuron** from Tregothnan really stood out – its wide open pink flowers set off with crimson spotting in the throat were an absolute delight. It is a species not often seen on the show benches and it appears now to be a member of Subsection Argyrophylla rather than Subsection Taliensia where it had been traditionally placed – such are the dynamics of rhododendron taxonomy!

A good specimen of **R. glischrum** was also on display – another plant rarely seen at shows.

RHODODENDRON GLISCHRUM

SALLY HAYWARD

The 'big-leaved' species were represented by a classic example of **R. falconeri ssp. _eximium_** with its persistent indumentum on the upper leaf surface and that distinctive pinkish flush to the flowers – a fine plant shown by Exbury.

Tregothnan exhibited a good full truss of **R. macabeanum**, grown under KW7724; its red stigmas contrasting beautifully with the primrose yellow corollas must surely make this collection the finest form of the species grown.

Regardless of its current status, the tender **R. parryae** (_R. roseatum_) caught the eyes and noses of the judges with its exquisite perfume and a full flawless truss. A regular in the Maddenia classes at the Main Rhododendron Competition, this truss was a treat for the Vincent Square visitor.

Amongst the hybrids on display, **_Rhododendron_ 'Ayesha'** was exhibited by Exbury. It was raised back in 1926 by Lionel de Rothschild from a cross between _R. fortunei_ ssp. _discolor_ and _R. arboreum_. Despite having been around for such a long time, it would appear difficult to improve upon its bright pink flowers borne in such large trusses, and it proves once again the admirable virtues of _R. arboreum_ as a parent.

RHODODENDRON FALCONERI SSP. *EXIMIUM*
SALLY HAYWARD

RHODODENDRON PARRYAE
SALLY HAYWARD

RHODODENDRON MACABEANUM KW7724
SALLY HAYWARD

R. ARGYROPHYLLUM X (SMIRNOWII X BUREAVII)

SALLY HAYWARD

R. 'AYESHA'   SALLY HAYWARD

R. FORMOSUM   SALLY HAYWARD

ROSEMOOR

It is remarkable that after such a severe winter there were almost 100 more rhododendrons entered into the Main Rhododendron Competition in 2011 than the year before. With 450 entries on the benches from which to choose, it was not without difficulty that the following were selected.

Maddenias can be difficult to keep in perfect condition in transit to the show but **Rhododendron formosum** is certainly one of the easiest and is a reliable and showy performer with the added attraction of finer foliage than most. It is a particularly good choice for the novice exhibitor.

Uncommon gems continue to appear from Trewithen and among them in 2011 was a gorgeous truss of the Reuthe hybrid **R. 'Soldier Sam'**. Raised from Dido Group x *dichroanthum*, it brings a distinctive colour to the show bench with superior foliage and a most attractive poise.

Selected in the southwest and with a reputation for flowering itself almost to the point of exhaustion, **R. 'Diana Colville'** is a much loved hybrid of R. *yunnanense*, although not in commerce. Its lavender tone with strong spotting is both fresh and pretty and in the garden it makes a statuesque but not imposing plant – it certainly deserved the FCC awarded in 1972. What a pity more of us aren't growing it.

R. 'SOLDIER SAM'   SALLY HAYWARD

It is an especial joy to be able to comment on **R. 'Lem's Cameo'** – on its first outing at a Rosemoor show. Another gem from Dido Group, this hybrid is pure gold if you can keep it well nourished – floriferous and healthy, with the most glorious trusses. It has both FCC and AGM awards yet is still relatively difficult to obtain, but well worth seeking out.

Marwood Hill Gardens are another source of hidden treasure. The late Dr Smart and his head gardener Malcolm Pharoah raised many interesting crosses from seed and some are just beginning to flower well enough to be assessed properly. Taking ones eye off the benches to admire the magnificent mass display presented by the garden, it was hard to ignore one particular rhododendron – an *argyrophyllum* x *(smirnowii* x *bureavii)* hybrid weighed down with beautifully marked, frilly white trusses. The distinctive foliage, although slightly marred by frost damage from an earlier bad winter, I suspect, shows real promise as a decorative feature in its own right and I look forward to this rhododendron being named, registered and brought into commerce.

On the magnolia competition benches, two entries caught my eye: **M. 'Sunburst'**, dazzling with its striking fresh, yellow flowers, and a sparkling pristine bloom of **M. 'Athene'**, one of the best Jury hybrids, in my opinion.

Contributions by Andy Simons, Ivor Stokes and Pam Hayward

R. 'DIANA COLVILLE' SALLY HAYWARD

R. 'LEM'S CAMEO' SALLY HAYWARD

MAGNOLIA 'SUNBURST' SALLY HAYWARD

MAGNOLIA 'ATHENE' SALLY HAYWARD

Tours

SCOTLAND
Rhododendron augustinii ssp. *hardyi*
at Benmore

Rhododendron augustinii, a lepidote from the Triflora subsection is usually seen in gardens and parks as a shrub with blue, lavender-blue or violet flowers. I was thrilled to see at Benmore a nicely shaped erect shrub, almost a small tree, with beautiful white flowers with bold yellowish-green blotches. The label revealed it to be *R. augustinii* ssp. *hardyi*. This rarely seen subspecies comes from East Tibet and North-West Yunnan and was introduced into cultivation in 1949.

RHODODENDRON *AUGUSTINII* SSP. *HARDYI* at Benmore
KRISTIAN THEQVIST

Rhododendron cerasinum
at Benmore and Crarae Garden

It is impossible to pass *Rhododendron cerasinum* without stopping to admire its striking, beautiful flowers. The species belongs to subsection Thomsonia and comes from South-East Tibet, Arunachal Pradesh and Upper Burma (Myanmar). There are two forms, named by Kingdon-Ward: the bi-coloured form is called 'Cherry Brandy' and the cherry-red form is 'Coals of Fire'. I could admire both forms in flower at Benmore. At Crarae Garden the path was ravishingly covered with cherry-red flowers from a large *R. cerasinum* and the pouring rain did not lessen the pleasure of seeing the colourful view.

RHODODENDRON CERASINUM 'COALS OF FIRE'
at Crarae Garden   KRISTIAN THEQVIST

Rhododendron cinnabarinum ssp. *tamaense* at Arduaine

Rhododendron cinnabarinum from subsection Cinnabarina is well known for its colourful, orange, red or yellow flowers. The rare subspecies ssp. *tamaense* from the Northern Triangle Temperate Forest of North Burma (Myanmar) is said to be leggy, not having particularly showy flowers and without garden merit. I disagree with this after seeing a magnificent specimen of *R. cinnabarinum* ssp. *tamaense* at Arduaine. The plant was full of tubular purple flowers.

RHODODENDRON CINNABARINUM SSP. TAMAENSE at Arduaine
KRISTIAN THEQVIST

Rhododendron oreotrephes at Achamore Gardens

Rhododendron oreotrephes is a very common lepidote from South East Tibet, Sichuan, North Yunnan and Burma (Myanmar), and it appears in many different forms. *R. oreotrephes* belongs to subsection Triflora but also has features that are typical of Cinnabarina. I have seen very floriferous large shrubs in gardens of Scandinavia and mainland Europe and I would not have chosen this species as an exceptional plant unless I had seen the handsome specimen at Achamore Gardens. There were not that many flowers on the small tree but the thick trunk covered with moss and the few scattered purple flowers made the scene something quite spectacular.

RHODODENDRON OREOTREPHES at Achamore Gardens
KRISTIAN THEQVIST

Garden Visits

A COOL HAVEN IN THE WOODLAND GARDEN AT GREENCOMBE where rhododendrons and azaleas blend perfectly with native trees, ferns and mosses
SALLY HAYWARD

GREENCOMBE

WITH EXMOOR JUST TO THE SOUTH and the full force of the Bristol Channel barely a mile to the north, Greencombe hardly sounds the most favoured location for a garden and yet its 3.5 acres are probably among the most sheltered in England.

Miss Joan Loraine has gardened here for nearly 50 years and her skills as a plantswoman and gardener are beyond doubt. Indeed, it is her deep and scholarly understanding of the natural processes at work in this garden which is at the root of its greatness, not to mention her legendary ability to manufacture vast quantities of leafmould!

Greencombe is a masterpiece of the exotic and native growing in perfect harmony to create a truly magical woodland garden.

Although there are four National Collections here – *Erythronium, Gaultheria, Polystichum* and *Vaccinium* – it is the rhododendrons and azaleas which provide the backbone to the woodland garden. Important among them are mature examples of the two most tender large-leaved species from subsection Grandia:

A SELF-SOWN *RHODODENDRON MAGNIFICUM* transplanted to a more suitable site
SALLY HAYWARD

THE MAGNIFICENT FOLIAGE OF
RHODODENDRON PROTISTUM

SALLY HAYWARD

This particular subspecies is well worth attempting for its foliage alone, highly decorative, glossy and more rounded than the rest of the subsection, with deeply impressed veins on the upper surface and coppery indumentum beneath. It has also proved an excellent parent, producing garden gems such as *R.* 'Gwilt King'.

Contributions by Kristian Theqvist and Pam Hayward

Rhododendron magnificum and *R. protistum*. Both flower prolifically here, very early in the year and are now, quite remarkably, self-seeding. Young plants have been transplanted through the woodland garden and the tropical quality of their foliage, completely unblemished by frost in 2011, adds to the general sense of wonder in this plantsman's heaven.

Both species are very difficult to grow elsewhere in most of the UK, being highly susceptible to frost, and specimens struggling in unfavourable locations are a miserable sight. Here at Greencombe, though, they can be properly admired as fine large trees, truly exceptional plants.

Another particular joy of this garden was a superb tree of *Rhododendron arboreum* **ssp.** *zeylanicum* absolutely ablaze with colour. The plentiful and perfect trusses of this plant provided further evidence of the benign microclimate of Greencombe.

THE GLORIOUS SIGHT OF *RHODODENDRON ARBOREUM* **SSP.** *ZEYLANICUM* in full bloom

SALLY HAYWARD

Challenge Cup Winners 2011

ALAN HARDY CHALLENGE SALVER

Awarded at the Early Rhododendron Competition to the exhibitor attaining the most points.
Mr John Anderson, Exbury Gardens

Three of the winning exhibits that contributed to the award

R. 'FIRST LIGHT'

SALLY HAYWARD

R. 'FORTUNE'

SALLY HAYWARD

R. 'CAREX'

SALLY HAYWARD

THE LIONEL DE ROTHSCHILD CHALLENGE CUP

The best exhibit of one truss of each of six species shown in Class 1 of the Main Rhododendron Competition.
Mr John Anderson, Exbury Gardens

Rhododendron arboreum
R. crinigerum
R. falconeri ssp. *eximium*
R. hyperythrum
R. rex ssp. *fictolacteum*
R. wightii

TOP ROW FROM LEFT: R. REX SSP. FICTOLACTEUM, R. FALCONERI SSP. EXIMIUM, R. WIGHTII BOTTOM ROW FROM LEFT: R. ARBOREUM, R. CRINIGERUM, R. HYPERYTHRUM

SALLY HAYWARD

THE MCLAREN CHALLENGE CUP

The best exhibit of any species of rhododendron, one truss shown in Class 3 of the Main Rhododendron Competition.
Mr Malcolm Pharoah Marwood Hill Gardens

Rhododendron sinofalconeri

RHODODENDRON SINOFALCONERI   SALLY HAYWARD

THE ROZA STEVENSON CHALLENGE CUP

The best exhibit of any species of rhododendron, one spray or branch with one or more than one truss shown in Class 4 of the Main Rhododendron Competition.
Mr John Anderson, Exbury Gardens

Rhododendron concinnum

RHODODENDRON CONCINNUM   SALLY HAYWARD

THE LODER CHALLENGE CUP

The best exhibit of any hybrid rhododendron, one truss shown in Class33 of the Main Rhododendron Competition.
Mrs Pat Bucknell

Rhododendron 'Horizon Monarch'

RHODODENDRON 'HORIZON MONARCH' SALLY HAYWARD

THE CROSFIELD CHALLENGE CUP

The best exhibit of three rhododendrons, raised by or in the garden of the exhibitor, one truss of each shown in Class 35 of the Main Rhododendron Competition.
Mr John Anderson, Exbury Gardens

Rhododendron 'Aurora', *Rhododendron* 'Hawk Crest' & *Rhododendron* 'Queen of Hearts'

R. 'AURORA'
SALLY HAYWARD

R. 'HAWK CREST'
SALLY HAYWARD

R. 'QUEEN OF HEARTS'
SALLY HAYWARD

THE LEONARDSLEE BOWL

The best exhibit of twelve cultivars of camellias, one bloom of each shown in Class 10 of the Main Camellia Competition
Mr Andrew Simons

Camellias:
'Annie Wylam'
'Anticipation'
'Augusto Pinto'
'Brigadoon'
'Desire'
'Interval'
'L. T. Dees'
'Lemon Drop'
'Owen Henry'
'Sugar Babe'
'Swan Lake'
'Takanini'

THE LEONARDSLEE BOWL   SALLY HAYWARD

BEST IN SHOW

(Wessex Branch Show at Ramster)
Mr Andy Fly

Rhododendron
'Kilimanjaro'

RHODODENDRON '**KILIMANJARO**'   JIM INSKIP

RHS Rhododendron & Camellia Sub-Committee

CHAIRMAN

MR A W SIMONS Wingfield House, 11 Brinsmade Road, Ampthill, Bedfordshire MK45 2PP
Email: a.simons@ntlworld.com

MEMBERS

MR P D EVANS West Netherton, Drewsteignton, Devon EX6 6RB
Email: philip.d.evans@talk21.com

MR M FLANAGAN Windsor Great Park, Windsor, Berkshire, SL4 2HT
Email: mark.flanagan@theroyallandscape.co.uk

MR M C FOSTER vmh White House Farm, Ivy Hatch, Sevenoaks, Kent TN15 0NN
Email: rosifoster@aol.com

MR J G HILLIER vmh c/o Hillier Nurseries Ltd, Ampfield House, Winchester Road, Ampfield
Romsey, Hampshire SO51 9PA
Email: john_hillier@hillier.co.uk

DR R H L JACK Edgemoor, 153 Hyndford Road, Lanark ML11 9BG

MR T METHUEN-CAMPBELL Penrice Castle, Oxwich, Swansea, West Glamorgan SA3 1LN
Email: trmmethuen@yahoo.co.uk

MR D G MILLAIS Millais Nurseries, Crosswater Farm, Churt, Farnham, Surrey GU10 2JN
Email: sales@rhododendrons.co.uk

MR M PHAROAH Lower Tithe Barn, Marwood Hill, Guineaford, Barnstaple, Devon EX31 4EB
Email: malcolmpharoah@btinternet.com

MR M O SLOCOCK vmh Hillside Cottage, Brentmoor Road, West End, Woking, Surrey GU24 9ND

MR C B TOMLIN Starborough Nursery, Starborough Road, Marsh Green, Edenbridge, Kent TN8 5RB
Email: starborough@hotmail.co.uk

MR C H WILLIAMS Burncoose Nurseries, Gwennap, Redruth, Cornwall TR16 6BJ
Email: diana@burncoose.co.uk

*During 2012 the committees of the Rhododendron & Camellia Sub-Committee and the
Rhododendron, Camellia & Magnolia Group will merge.*

Rhododendron, Camellia & Magnolia Group

OFFICERS

CHAIRMAN
MR ANDY SIMONS Wingfield House, 11 Brinsmade Road, Ampthill, Bedfordshire MK45 2PP
Tel: 01525 753398 Email: a.simons@ntlworld.com

VICE CHAIRMAN
MR PHILIP D EVANS West Netherton, Drewsteignton, Devon EX6 6RB
Tel/Fax: 01647 281285 (phone first) Email: philip.d.evans@talk21.com

HON. TREASURER
MR ALASTAIR T STEVENSON Appledore, Upton Bishop, Ross-on-Wye, Herefordshire HR9 7UL
Tel: 01989 780285 Fax: 01989 780591 Email: alastairstevenson@mpaconsulting.co.uk

HON. SECRETARY
MRS PAT BUCKNELL Botallick, Lanreath, Looe, Cornwall PL13 2PF
Tel: 01503 220215 Email: patbucknell@btinternet.com

HON. MEMBERSHIP SECRETARY
MR RUPERT L C ELEY East Bergholt Place, East Bergholt, Suffolk CO7 6UP
Tel: 01206 299224 Fax: 01206 299229 Email: sales@placeforplants.co.uk

HON. YEARBOOK EDITOR & ARCHIVIST
PAM HAYWARD Woodtown, Sampford Spiney, Yelverton, Devon PL20 6LJ
Tel/Fax: 01822 852122 Email: pam@woodtown.net

HON. BULLETIN EDITOR
MR JOHN RAWLING The Spinney, Station Road, Woldingham, Surrey CR3 7DD
Tel: 01883 653341 Email: jr.eye@virgin.net

HON. TOURS ORGANISER
MRS JUDY HALLETT The Old Rectory, Thruxton, Herefordshire HR2 9AX
Tel: 01981 570401 Email: judy.hallett@googlemail.com

WEBMASTER
MR GRAHAM MILLS Tregoning Mill, St. Keverne, Helston, Cornwall TR12 6QE
Tel: 01326 280382 Fax: 0871 433 7066 Email: graham@tregoningmill.co.uk

COMMITTEE MEMBERS

MR ERIC ANNAL 36 Hillview Crescent, Edinburgh EH12 8QG
Tel: 0131 334 2574 Fax: 0131 334 6191 Email: eric.annal@btinternet.com

MR JOHN D HARSANT Newton House, Well Lane, Heswall, Wirral CH60 8NF
Tel: 0151 342 3664 Fax: 0151 348 4015 Email: john@harsant.uk.com (Publicity Officer)

MR STEPHEN LYUS 11 Meadway, Spital, Wirral CH62 2AR
Tel: 0151 200 0265 Email: emailslyus@yahoo.co.uk (Advertising Officer)

Mr THOMAS METHUEN-CAMPBELL Penrice Castle, Oxwich, Swansea, West Glamorgan SA3 1LN
Tel: 01792 390008 Fax: 01792 391081 Email: trmmethuen@yahoo.co.uk

MRS CHERYL SAPCOTE 103 Quinton Lane, Quinton, Birmingham B32 2TT
Tel: 0121 423 3949 Email: cherylsapcote@btinternet.com

MR IVOR T STOKES Llyshendy, Llandeilo, Carmarthenshire SA19 6YA
Tel/Fax: 01558 823233 Email: ivor.t.stokes@btopenworld.com

BRANCH CHAIRMEN

INTERNATIONAL
MRS MIRANDA GUNN Ramster, Chiddingfold, Surrey GU8 4SN
Tel: 01428 644422 Email: miranda@ramstergardens.com

NEW FOREST
MR JOHN G HILLIER vMH c/o Hillier Nurseries Ltd, Ampfield House, Ampfield, Romsey, Hampshire SO51 9PA Email: john_hillier@hillier.co.uk

NORFOLK
Vacancy

NORTH WALES/NORTHWEST
MR C E J BRABIN Rosewood, Puddington Village, Neston CH64 5SS
Tel: 0151 353 1193 Email: angela.brabin@btinternet.com

PEAK
DR. DAVID R IVES 18 Park Road, Birstall, Leicestershire LE4 3AU
Tel: 0116 267 5118 Email: dandrives@talktalk.net

SOUTHEAST
MR BARRY HASELTINE Goodwins, Snow Hill, Crawley Down, Sussex RH10 3EF
Tel: 01342 713132 Email: barry.haseltine@which.net

SOUTHWEST
MR COLIN H T BROWN West Winds, Lustleigh, Newton Abbot, Devon TQ13 9TR
Tel: 01647 277268 Email: marylou@lustleigh.plus.com

ULSTER
Vacancy

WESSEX
MRS MIRANDA GUNN Ramster, Chiddingfold, Surrey GU8 4SN
Tel: 01428 644422 Fax: 01428 658345 Email: miranda@ramstergardens.com

WEST MIDLANDS
MR ALASTAIR T STEVENSON Appledore, Upton Bishop, Ross-on-Wye, Herefordshire HR9 7UL
Tel: 01989 780285 Fax: 01989 780591 Email: AlastairStevenson@mpaconsulting.co.uk

CONVENOR OF GROUP SEED BANK

MRS MARGARET MILES Trewollack, St Mawes, Truro, Cornwall TR2 5AD
Tel: 01326 270229 Email: margaret@trewollack.co.uk

WEBSITE

www.rhodogroup-rhs.org

MAGNOLIA STELLATA 'JANE PLATT'
SALLY HAYWARD

Index

National RHS Rhododendron Show

Reg. Charity No. 222879/SC038262

Saturday 21 April & Sunday 22 April
10am - 4pm

RHS Garden Rosemoor
Great Torrington Devon EX38 8PH
Tel: 01805 624067
www.rhs.org.uk/rosemoor

Royal
Horticultural
Society

MILLAIS NURSERIES

Crosswater Farm
Crosswater Lane
Church
Farnham
Surrey
GU10 2JN
01252 792698

Specialist Growers of Rhododendrons and Azaleas

We grow one of the finest ranges of Rhododendrons and Azaleas in the country. Everything from historic varieties rescued from some of the great plant collections, to the latest introductions from around the world.

Sun Fire
Luscious flame orange flowers on a compact plant in May.

Double Dots
Double pale pink flowers with a profusion of dark red dots.

Autumn Magic (Herbstzauber
Deep pink yak hybrid with red markin flowering in May and Autumn.

RHS Chelsea Flower Show Gold Medal and
'Plant of the Year' Finalist (*R. Rabatz*) 2011. We are the best!

Fantastic searchable website with secure online payment.

Fast and acclaimed delivery throughout Europe.

Quality specimen plants available up to 1.5m high.

Plant Centre hours: Monday to Friday 10am–5pm
Saturdays in Spring and Autumn

See us at the 2012 National Rhododendron Show, Rosemoor 21–22 April

www.rhododendrons.co.uk
sales@rhododendrons.co.uk